Jonathan P. Tomes, J.D.

Industry Regulation

Other Books in the Guide for the Healthcare Professional Series

Antitrust Law, by Jonathan P. Tomes, 1993

Environmental Law, by Jonathan P. Tomes, 1993

Fraud, Waste, Abuse and Safe Harbors, by Jonathan P. Tomes, 1993

Healthcare EDI, by James J. Moynihan, 1993

Jonathan P. Tomes, J.D.

Industry Regulation

A Guide for
the Healthcare
Professional

PROBUS PUBLISHING COMPANY
Chicago, Illinois
Cambridge, England

 HEALTHCARE FINANCIAL MANAGEMENT ASSOCIATION

HFMA gratefully acknowledges the gracious assistance of the following content reviewers for this book: Connie Cape, FHFMA, CPA; Paul DeMuro, FHFMA, CMPA, CPA, J.D.; Warren Hern, FHFMA; R. R. Kovener, FHFMA; Marvin Kurtz, FHFMA, CMPA, CPA; and Clifford Ogborn, FHFMA, CPA.

Copyright © 1993 by Healthcare Financial Management Association
FIRST EDITION
FIRST PRINTING—1993

All rights reserved. No part of this publication may be reproduced, stored in a retrieval system, or transmitted, in any form or by any means, electronic, mechanical, photocopying, recording, or otherwise, without the prior written permission of the copyright owner.

Although every precaution has been taken in the preparation of this book, the publisher and author assume no responsibility for errors or omissions. Neither is any liability assumed for damages resulting from the use of the information contained herein.

Printed in the United States of America

Library of Congress Cataloging-in-Publication Data

Tomes, Jonathan P.
    The healthcare financial manager's guide to healthcare industry regulation / by Jonathan P. Tomes.
       p. cm. — (Healthcare financial manager's library)
    Includes bibliographical references and index.
    ISBN 1-882198-00-X $37.95
    1. Health facilities—Law and legislation—United States.
    2. Health facilities—United States—Business management.
    I. Title. II. Series
KF3825.T655   1993
344.73'0321—dc20
[347.304321]

92-35485
CIP

10 9 8 7 6 5 4 3 2 1

Contents

Chapter 1: An Overview of the Legal Status of the Healthcare Industry, 1

Government Justification for Healthcare Regulation, 1
Implications of Increased Regulation for Healthcare Facilities, 4

Chapter 2: The Legal Basis for Government Regulation of Health Care, 7

State Authority to Regulate Health Care, 7
Federal Authority to Regulate Health Care, 8
How Does the Government Exercise Its Powers?, 14

Chapter 3: Regulation of Healthcare Facilities by Organizational Statutes, 17

Business Organizations, 17
Alternative Delivery Systems, 21

Chapter 4: Regulation Through Licensure, 25

Licensing of Healthcare Professionals, 25

Facility Licensure, 29
Certificates of Need, 32

Chapter 5: Private Regulation, 35
The Joint Commission on the Accreditation of Healthcare Organizations, 35
Other Private Regulatory Organizations, 40

Chapter 6: Self-Regulation, 43
Articles of Incorporation and Bylaws, 43
The Governing Board, 45
The Facility Administrator, 47
The Medical Staff, 48

Chapter 7: Judicial Regulation of the Healthcare Industry, 53
An Overview of the Judicial System, 53
Malpractice Litigation, 57

Chapter 8: Regulation Through Taxation, 63
Charitable Purposes, 64
Unrelated Business Income, 67
Private Inurement, 69
Restrictions on Lobbying and Campaign Activities, 71
Regulation of For-Profit Entities Through Taxation, 71

Chapter 9: Critical Issues in Healthcare Regulation, 73
AIDS Issues, 73
Antitrust Issues, 74
Environmental and Occupational Safety and Health Issues, 75
Medicare and Medicaid Issues, 75
Other Issues, 76
Conclusion, 76

Glossary, 79

Bibliography, 85

Index, 89

About the Author, 95

An Overview of the Legal Status of the Healthcare Industry

Hospitals and other healthcare facilities are among the most extensively regulated institutions in the United States.[1] They are regulated by all levels of government—federal, state, and local—and by numerous agencies within each level.[2] In addition, various private organizations, such as the Joint Commission on the Accreditation of Healthcare Organizations (JCAHO), regulate healthcare facilities. Internally, hospitals are regulated by their bylaws.

To better understand the importance of the current regulatory climate, financial managers should understand the justifications for governmental regulation of the healthcare industry and the implications of this regulation for the financial health of the facility.

❖ Government Justification for Healthcare Regulation

Much of this pervasive governmental regulation is the result of the healthcare environment in which hospitals and other facil-

---

1. Arthur Levin, "The Search for New Forms of Control," in *Regulating Health Care: The Struggle for Control* (New York: Academy of Political Science, 1980), p. 1.
2. Robert Miller, *Problems in Hospital Law* (Rockville, Md.: Aspen Systems Corp., 1983), p. 45 (hereinafter, Miller).

ities operate today. Previously, the chief concern of regulators of the healthcare industry was ensuring the quality of healthcare services. In recent years, however, healthcare regulation has been increasingly concerned with the cost of health care.[3]

Regulation of the quality of health care includes licensing of healthcare professionals, licensing of healthcare facilities, quality control (risk management and quality assurance) activities, professional liability (malpractice law), and others.

However, the growth of third-party payment and the change in medical practice from an emphasis on generalists to increasing reliance on specialists—with a concomitant increase in the use of expensive new diagnostic and therapeutic techniques and equipment—have led to rapid increases in the cost of medical care. The escalation of healthcare costs has been accompanied by a corresponding increase in healthcare regulations to contain these costs. Healthcare cost control regulation includes, for example, health planning and certificates of need, rate regulation, Medicare and Medicaid fraud and abuse laws, the Medicare Utilization and Quality Peer Review (PRO) program, and laws designed to encourage more efficient provider organizations, among others.

Governments have traditionally used several economic and political justifications for their regulatory efforts. Many government interventions are based on perceived imperfections on the supply side of some specific economic market. Because of economies of scale (in theory, bigger facilities are more efficient), consumers may have only one supplier of a given healthcare service, and that monopolistic vendor therefore can charge a high price.[4]

In addition, the market for some healthcare professionals, particularly physicians, has been uncompetitive. Entry into the market is severely restricted, including limited access to and high cost of medical education and the necessity of obtaining licenses and private certifications. Because physicians largely direct the consumption of their own services, they may actually generate demand for

---

3. Barry R. Furrow, Sandra H. Johnson, Timothy S. Jost, and Robert L. Schwartz, *Health Law: Cases, Materials, and Problems,* 2d ed. (St. Paul, Minn.: West Publishing Co., 1991), p. 661 (hereinafter, Furrow et al.).
4. Penny Feldman and Marc Roberts, "Magic Bullets or Seven Card Stud: Understanding Health Care Regulation," in Richard S. Gordon, ed., *Issues in Health Care Regulation* (New York: McGraw-Hill Book Co., 1980), p. 66 (hereinafter, Feldman and Roberts).

their services, thus raising prices. Further, supply distortions have resulted from hospitals not behaving competitively. Hospitals may compete more directly for physicians than for patients because physicians produce patients. Competing for physicians has led to inefficiencies by causing hospitals to purchase expensive and perhaps unnecessary equipment to attract physicians, thereby raising costs. In addition, the nonprofit status of many hospitals may not lead to the efficiencies that a profit motive would generate.[5] These and other supply distortions have led to such government interventions as price control regulations and antitrust laws.

The government also justifies regulation based on perceived inadequacies on the demand side of the market, usually by deeming consumers unwilling or unable to make informed and appropriate choices.[6] Patients "purchase" healthcare services differently than they buy a new car. They typically have little time to research medical options and little experience with ways to make an informed choice about the most appropriate treatment. Rather, they rely on physicians to make medical services purchases for them. Physicians direct the expenditure of approximately 70 cents of every healthcare dollar. Thus, they, rather than their patients, are in effect the true purchasers of healthcare services. And physicians are trained to provide necessary medical care, largely regardless of the cost.

Further, insofar as the patient might otherwise be concerned about the cost, the widespread use of third-party payers makes the cost of necessary medical treatment a fairly minor concern to the patient. And if insurance pays for all or most of a medical service, the patient's decision is essentially whether to "purchase" a free good, thereby inducing a demand-side distortion that results in increased healthcare costs. Although insurers have an incentive to reduce costs, they have traditionally chosen to pass increased costs on to their insureds rather than aggressively attempt to control costs.[7] Again, the government attempts to regulate demand distortions by encouraging innovative forms of practice that may cut

---

5. Furrow et al., p. 665.
6. Feldman and Roberts, p. 66.
7. Furrow et al., pp. 662-64.

costs and by such laws as the Medicare and Medicaid fraud and abuse laws and the Medicare PRO program.

Of course, supply and demand are interrelated. For example, the imperfections of patient decision making on the one hand and the dynamics of the supply side on the other lead to a situation in which "supply creates its own demand," that is, "A bed built is a bed filled is a bed billed."[8] Governments have responded to this supply-and-demand distortion by requiring certificates of need (CON), which require healthcare institutions to demonstrate a need to expand or acquire new healthcare technology to obtain the government's consent to a purchase.

❖ Implications of Increased Regulation for Healthcare Facilities

This pervasive regulation has tremendous implications for the financial viability of all healthcare facilities. Complying with the myriad governmental laws and regulations alone can significantly affect the financial health of your facility. Yet not complying may be much worse. As one healthcare financial management expert has noted:

> Regulation in its various forms can significantly affect income and cash flow and, therefore, financial viability. For example, if a hospital has been mandated to upgrade certain facilities by a regulatory agency, the cost of such renovation must be taken into account in calculating future cash flow, and the impact on cash flow will depend on the amount of added cost as well as the method by which the improvements are financed. Similarly, if new regulations require a hospital's department to hire new types of highly skilled, licensed staff, the department's expenses and cash flow could markedly change. . . . If the viability of a hospital business is tied to its ability to generate future net cash flow, these regulatory costs—both operating and capital costs—must be taken into account.[9]

---

8. Ruth Roemer, "Bed Supply and Hospital Utilization: A Natural Experiment," *Hospitals 1961* U.S. 35 (November 1, 1961), p. 37.
9. James Unland, *The Trustee's Guide to Understanding Hospital Business Fundamentals* (Westchester, Ill.: Healthcare Financial Management Association, 1991), pp. 34-35.

This book will help you understand the healthcare regulatory environment by explaining how both the federal and state governments and private organizations regulate the industry and how facilities regulate themselves. Chapter 2 discusses the legal basis for government regulation. The remaining chapters cover specific areas of government regulation.

The Legal Basis for Government Regulation of Health Care

We have grown so used to government regulation that we seldom think about whether, and under what authority, the government is regulating an industry such as health care. We tend to assume that the government is responsible for almost everything, but in a government of laws, the government must have a legal basis for any regulation it undertakes.[1] Ultimately, both the states and the federal government derive their authority to regulate health care from the United States Constitution. This chapter will first discuss state authority to regulate health care, then contrast that authority with that of the federal government. Next, the chapter examines limitations on governmental ability to regulate health care. Finally, the text reviews the instrumentalities through which the government exercises its power to regulate the industry.

❖ State Authority to Regulate Health Care

The states have the authority to regulate hospitals under the police power. The police power is the inherent power of state gov-

---

1. Steven M. Fleisher, "The Law of Basic Public Health Activities: Police Power and Constitutional Limitations," in Ruth Roemer and George McKray, eds., *Legal Aspects of Health Policy, Issues and Trends* (Westport, Conn.: Greenwood, 1980), p. 4.

ernments to impose restrictions on individuals or entities that are reasonably related to the promotion and the maintenance of the health, safety, morals, and general welfare of the public. The source of this power is the Tenth Amendment to the United States Constitution, which reserves to the states or to the people any powers not specifically given to the federal government by that document.

A state's regulation of healthcare institutions must further the health, safety, and general welfare of its citizens.[2] In the public health area, the police power most often regulates

- licensing and inspection of health facilities
- establishment of public hospitals and clinics
- pest control, sanitation, and sewage rules
- communicable disease control and prevention
- regulation of drugs
- employee health and safety rules
- gathering of vital statistics[3]

In summary, each state has sweeping powers to regulate the healthcare industry under the state's police power. These powers are limited only by the specific authority granted to the federal government by the U.S. Constitution, which preempts state authority, and the protection of individual rights under both the federal and state constitutions.

❖ Federal Authority to Regulate Health Care

In contrast to the states' broad police power to regulate health care, the federal government's authority comes mainly from its role as the purchaser of health care.[4] In 1990, the federal government spent approximately 196 billion dollars on medical care. As a purchaser, the federal government regulates by certifying healthcare

---

2. Furrow et al., p. 78.
3. *Id.*, p. 29.
4. *Id.*, p. 87.

providers. In order to receive payments under Medicare or Medicaid, a healthcare provider must be certified and sign a provider agreement.

The U.S. Constitution does not specifically empower the federal government to regulate health care. The only provisions of the Constitution that provide a basis for regulating health care are the Interstate Commerce Clause and the taxing power. For example, the government initiated programs in the 1800s to establish quarantines to control cholera and yellow fever epidemics. These programs were justified because epidemics were spread through interstate commerce, which the federal government could regulate under the Commerce Clause.[5]

The federal government also regulates under the power to tax by, for example, taking away nonprofit entities' tax-exempt status if they do not adhere to specific rules.[6] As employers, healthcare facilities are subject to regulation under the Internal Revenue Code with respect to such items as employment taxes and retirement benefits. In addition, the tax laws play a major role in healthcare facility financing.

Limitations on Governmental Authority to Regulate Healthcare

Although both the federal and the state governments enjoy broad powers to regulate health care, such powers are not unlimited. The federal government can only exercise those powers granted to it by the U.S. Constitution. State police power must, as discussed previously, further the health, safety, and general welfare of its citizens.

Although the states derive their police power from the Tenth Amendment to the U.S. Constitution, the Constitution limits the exercise of that power if it conflicts with a legitimate federal power. Article VI of the Constitution, known as the *supremacy clause*, specifies that in any matter in which state action is incompatible with federal actions, the state action is "preempted" by the federal. For

---

5. *Id.*, p. 34.
6. *Id.*, p. 507.

example, in North Carolina v. Califano,[7] the Supreme Court upheld the constitutionality of the certificate-of-need (CON) provisions of a federal statute against a state claim that, under state law, the state could not implement the federal CON requirement and would lose the right to participate in federal financial assistance programs. Under the supremacy clause, the federal statute prevailed over the state law. Thus, if a state healthcare law or regulation conflicts with a federal one, the latter prevails. For example, a state statute that conflicted with the federal Civil Rights Act of 1964[8] would not be enforceable. Similarly, in Alexander v. Choate,[9] the handicapped plaintiffs argued that the state's decision to cover only 14 days of inpatient care per recipient per fiscal year discriminated against the handicapped under § 504 of the Rehabilitation Act of 1973[10] because the handicapped, on the average, require more inpatient care. The Supreme Court rejected this claim because the state requirement was neutral on its face and provided the handicapped and nonhandicapped with an equally accessible benefit.

Both the federal and the state governments are limited by the rights guaranteed to individuals (and, by extension, to entities) by both the federal and state constitutions. Most of the provisions of the Bill of Rights may, by their terms, be a constraint on the federal government's regulation of health care. By virtue of the Fourteenth Amendment, which extends the operation of the Bill of Rights to the states, they likewise cannot regulate health care in a manner that violates a protection given by the Bill of Rights. Specific protections of the Constitution that may limit government regulation of the healthcare industry include the factors described next.

Due Process Both the Fifth and Fourteenth Amendments contain a due process clause. The Fifth Amendment due process clause reads, "[N]or shall any person . . . be deprived of life, liberty, or property, without due process of law; nor shall private property be taken for public use, without just compensation." No one has

---

7. 435 U.S. 96 (1978).
8. 42 U.S.C. § 2000d (1992).
9. 469 U.S. 287 (1985).
10. 29 U.S.C. § 794 (1992).

ever defined due process precisely, but "fundamental fairness" is as good a definition as any. It means that the government may not take a person's (corporations may be considered "persons" for some constitutional protections) life, liberty, or property without affording that person notice of the proposed action and an opportunity to be heard as to why the government should not take the action. Due process is a flexible concept—the amount of due process the government must provide depends on how serious the action is. The more severe the deprivation, the more rights the government must afford. In very serious cases, such as those involving incarceration, the right to be heard may include the following rights:

- to present evidence
- to compel the presence of witnesses
- to confront (see, hear, and cross-examine) adverse witnesses
- to be heard by an unbiased decision maker
- to have the assistance of counsel
- to make an appeal[11]

For example, in Klein v. Califano,[12] the court held that residents of a federally funded nursing home had a right to a hearing before any decision to terminate the nursing home's eligibility for Medicaid funds because they had a property interest in their right to

---

11. *See, for example,* Goldberg v. Kelly, 397 U.S. 254 (1970). The rights required by due process before an administrative agency include the rights to
- Notice, including an adequate formulation of the subjects and issues involved in the case.
- Present evidence (both testimonial and documentary) and argument.
- Rebut adverse evidence, through cross-examination and other appropriate means.
- Appear with counsel.
- Have the decision based only upon evidence introduced into the record of the hearing.
- Have a complete record, which consists of a transcript of the testimony and arguments, together with the documentary evidence and all papers filed in the proceeding.

From Bernard Schwartz, *Administrative Law*, 2d ed. (Boston and Toronto: Little, Brown & Co., 1984), pp. 203-4.

12. 586 F.2d 250 (3d Cir. 1978).

continued occupancy in the nursing home because the Medicaid law limited the conditions for which a resident can be transferred.

Equal Protection The Fourteenth Amendment adds to the due process clause the equal protection clause, "nor [shall any State] deny to any person within its jurisdiction the equal protection of the laws." Equal protection is an extremely complicated area of the law, but, simplistically stated, it prevents treating persons differently for no good reason. If a group is treated differently because of a "suspect classification," such as race, the state must prove a compelling governmental interest that can only be accomplished by taking the action in question.

An example of an equal protection violation affecting healthcare regulations occurred in Hathaway v. Worcester County Hospital.[13] In this case, the court found that a hospital's ban on nontherapeutic sterilization violated the equal protection rights of patients seeking such treatments, because the facility routinely performed procedures of equal risk and complexity and could not provide a rational basis for the ban. Note that the facility was a county hospital—the Bill of Rights generally does not apply to purely private actions.

Similarly, in Memorial Hospital v. Maricopa County,[14] the U.S. Supreme Court struck down a state law that prohibited indigent citizens from obtaining emergency care in county facilities until they had resided in the county for one year. The state's interests in saving money, administrative convenience, and preventing fraud were not sufficient as a defense against an equal protection attack, because the state could accomplish these goals through means that did not infringe on the right of interstate travel.

Freedom of Speech The First Amendment's protection of freedom of speech means that individuals have the right to express their thoughts without governmental restrictions on the contents thereof. How could freedom of speech involve health care? In Virginia State Board of Pharmacy v. Virginia Citizens Consumer Council, Inc.,[15] the court noted that the state ban on advertising of pre-

---

13. 475 F.2d 701 (1st Cir. 1973).
14. 415 U.S. 250 (1974).
15. 425 U.S. 748 (1976).

scription drug prices violated the First Amendment's guarantee of freedom of speech. A state may restrict "commercial speech"—advertising—as to time, place, and manner but may not ban it altogether.

Freedom from Unreasonable Searches and Seizures The Fourth Amendment protects against unreasonable searches and seizures. In Marshall v. Barlow's Inc.,[16] the Supreme Court held that the Fourth Amendment's warrant requirement applies to commercial buildings as well as to private homes. The Fourth Amendment may apply in other healthcare contexts as well. For example, in Carlton v. Herschel,[17] the court found that a doctor had immunity against a claim he violated the plaintiff's rights when he removed a bullet from the plaintiff's chest pursuant to a search warrant. Although a magistrate found that there was a sufficiently close connection between the physician's actions and the search warrant so that the act of removing the bullet was a state action, the physician was entitled to assert a good faith defense that he was acting pursuant to a valid search warrant. The Sixth Circuit Court of Appeals agreed with the district court that the magistrate erroneously found state action but agreed with the dismissal of the suit. Similarly, Rodreiques v. Furtado[18] noted that it would not require a physician to look behind an objectively reasonable and facially valid warrant to determine whether it was based on probable cause.

In another healthcare case, the U.S. Supreme Court held that a state-run hospital did not need a warrant to search the office, desk, and file drawers of a doctor who was on leave of absence pending an investigation of alleged misconduct. The reason was that requiring an employer to obtain a warrant to enter an employee's office, desk, or file cabinets for a work-related purpose would seriously disrupt the routine conduct of business and be unduly burdensome.[19]

Finally, Kemp v. Claiborne County Hospital[20] addressed the question whether a hospital could terminate employment of a scrub

---

16. 436 U.S. 307 (1978).
17. 1991 LEXIS 1599 (6th Cir. 1991).
18. 950 F.2d 805 (1st Cir. 1991).
19. O'Connor v. Ortega, 107 S.Ct. 1492 (1987).
20. 763 F. Supp. 1362 (S.D. Miss. 1991).

technician in surgery when she refused to give a urine sample as a part of the hospital's mandatory drug testing program. The plaintiff contended that the collection and testing of her urine by the publicly owned hospital was an unreasonable search under the Constitution. The court used a balancing test, weighing the plaintiff's privacy interest against the hospital's interest. The court found the hospital's interest in safety—that patients should not have to bear the risk that employees who might suffer from impaired perception and judgment due to drug or alcohol abuse would occupy positions in which they are responsible for the care and treatment of patients—outweighed the plaintiff's interests. The court also noted that the testing procedures used by the facility minimized the intrusiveness of collecting the urine samples.[21]

❖ How Does the Government Exercise Its Powers?

In our system of government, governmental power is divided among three branches—the executive, the legislative, and the judicial, each of which is intended to act as a check on one of the others accumulating too much power. The Congress, as the legislative branch, regulates health care, as well as other areas, by enacting statutes that become effective when the president, as head of the executive branch, signs them into law. Of course, the Congress can override a presidential veto and thereby put a law into effect itself. The laws enacted by Congress typically set broad policy guidance and leave the details of implementing the policy to administrative agencies. The executive branch is responsible for executing the laws. It normally does so through administrative agencies, such as the U.S. Department of Health and Human Services.

Executive agencies make law in two ways: by promulgating regulations implementing the guidance contained in the statutes

---

21. Factors cited to lessen the intrusiveness of urine collection include
    ❖ Collecting it in a medical-type environment.
    ❖ Having trained medical personnel collect the samples.
    ❖ Making the procedures similar to those required for regular physical examinations.
    ❖ Making no requirement for the test monitor to observe the employee as he or she produces the urine sample.

enacted by the Congress and by adjudicating disputes between parties regulated by the agency. Of course an agency may propose legislation to be enacted by the legislature. More often, however, the agency will promulgate regulations governing the area in question. Such rulemaking power is "quasi-legislative" in that the agency's rules have the same force of law as if the Congress or a state legislature had enacted them in a statute as long as they do not conflict with the Constitution or a statute and the agency complies with the procedural requirements for rulemaking.

Adjudication is nothing more than resolving a dispute between the agency and another party or between two parties in an administrative hearing rather than before a court. If the legislature gives the agency the power to adjudicate, its decisions have the same force of law as do court decisions. Thus, a decision by an agency administrative law judge that required a healthcare facility that was a party to the adjudication to, for example, improve its medical charting, maintain employee health records, and correct staffing deficiencies or face suspension of its license,[22] would set a precedent that should require others similarly situated to do so as well.

One other aspect of agency powers is important. Most agencies have the power to investigate the persons or organizations that they regulate. The power to investigate usually carries with it the authority to subpoena documents and to inspect premises.

Not only do administrative agencies interpret and detail the law through promulgating regulations, they enforce it through sanctions such as fines, suspension, or revocation of licensure, or even referring the matter for prosecution as a criminal matter.

The courts, of course, are the branch of government primarily responsible for interpreting the laws. Violations of government laws and regulations may be prosecuted as criminal matters or as civil matters. And both the government and private and public entities may sue to redress their rights under federal and state constitutions, laws, and regulations. Even though agencies may also decide cases in agency adjudications, court decisions are greater

---

22. *See* Thompson v. Division of Health of Missouri, 604 S.W.2d 802 (Mo. Ct. App. 1980).

authority than agency decisions, just as the legislature's statutes are greater authority than administrative regulations.

As you can see, both the federal and state governments (including local governments) have the power, under the states' and U.S. Constitutions, to regulate the healthcare industry, subject to Constitutional and other limitations.

Regulation of Healthcare Facilities by Organizational Statutes

We often do not think about the government setting requirements concerning the corporate structure of a healthcare facility as a means of regulating that facility. However, a hospital or other healthcare facility must meet state requirements—such as minimum capital, filing of articles of incorporation, and so forth—to incorporate or qualify for some other status, such as a professional association or a partnership. After defining the common business organizations healthcare providers are organized as, this chapter discusses governmental requirements for professional organizations and alternate delivery organizations.

❖ Business Organizations

A *corporation* is an association of shareholders created under state law. The courts regard this association as an artificial person having a legal entity entirely separate and distinct from the individuals who compose it, with the capacity of continuous existence and the capacity to exercise such powers as are not illegal or as otherwise limited by the articles of incorporation. A corporation may sue or be sued as an entity and may hold property in its corporate name. Shareholders are not generally liable for any obligations of the corporation except to the extent of their investment.

Many different types of corporations exist: for-profit, not-for-profit, municipal, private, and public, among others. Most hospitals and many other healthcare facilities are organized as either for-profit or not-for-profit corporations. For-profit hospitals are in business to earn profits and may pay income to their shareholders who are entitled to dividends awarded by the boards of directors and to share in the assets of the corporations. A not-for-profit corporation may earn a "profit," although that is not the corporation's primary purpose. Rather, it is organized to render a service. A not-for-profit corporation may not distribute its income to members, directors, or officers other than the payment of reasonable compensation for services rendered. A nonprofit corporation may not distribute dividends to its members (the equivalent of shareholders) but rather must use any "profits"—the excess of income over expenses—for its charitable purposes.

An *association* is a collection of persons who have joined together for a certain purpose. When people join together to form an association, that entity has legal rights and obligations. It may, for example, depending on its form and upon state law, sue or be sued or may be able to enter into contracts.

Associations may take differing forms, depending on their purpose and the laws of the jurisdictions they operate in. Associations may be incorporated or unincorporated and may be for-profit or not-for-profit. Depending on the association's structure and the law of the state in which the association operates, the courts may treat an unincorporated association as a partnership or other legal entity, such as a syndicate or a trust. Or a state statute may give a particular type of association, such as a medical association, a specific status as outlined in the relevant statute. Most states do, however, provide for the incorporation of associations.

A *partnership* is a business arrangement in which two or more persons join together and agree to divide the profit and bear the loss of the business in certain proportions. Partners are individually liable for the debts of the partnership, and creditors may seek and recover the partners' individual assets when the assets of the partnership are insufficient to satisfy the creditors.

Professional Corporations and Associations

Virtually all states have now enacted professional corporation acts. Generally, the acts provide that such corporate shareholders are only liable to the extent of their investment in the corporation and personal liability is limited to a shareholder's own negligent acts or those of subordinate employees he or she supervised or controlled. In addition, creditors of a small corporation often require that the shareholders personally guarantee its debts. Generally, states require shareholders to be licensed to practice the profession, limit the corporation's business to that profession, and impose limitations on the transfer of corporate stock.[1] The requirements for doing business as such a professional corporation constitute a significant form of regulation of the healthcare industry.

In Illinois, for example, one or more physicians licensed under the Medical Practice Act may form a medical corporation.[2] Medical services may be rendered by employees of such a corporation only if they are licensed under the Medical Practice Act. Further, only persons licensed under the act may be officers, directors, or shareholders. Except where a conflict exists, in which case the Medical Practice Act controls, the Business Corporation Act[3] governs the organization and functioning of a medical corporation.

Prior to commencing business, an Illinois medical corporation must obtain a certificate of registration from the state's department of registration and education. The certificate must be renewed annually and may be revoked for violations of the law. The department will issue a certificate if it finds that

- ❖ The incorporators, officers, directors, and shareholders of the corporation are properly licensed under the Medical Practice Act.
- ❖ No disciplinary action is pending before the department regarding any of the incorporators, officers, directors, or shareholders.

---

1. Furrow et al., p. 526.
2. Ill. Rev. Stat. ch. 32, ¶ 632 (1985).
3. Ill. Rev. Stat. ch. 32, ¶ 1.01, et seq. (1985).

❖ It appears that the corporation will be conducted in accordance with the law, including the department's regulations.

The department may revoke or suspend the certificate, which must be renewed annually, for any of the following reasons:

❖ The revocation or suspension of the license to practice medicine of any officer, director, shareholder, or employee of the corporation if the corporation does not promptly remove or discharge such person.
❖ The commission of unethical professional conduct on the part of any officer, director, shareholder, or employee of the corporation, when the corporation does not promptly remove or discharge such a person.
❖ The death of the sole remaining shareholder of the corporation.
❖ A finding that the corporation has failed to comply with provisions of the Medical Corporation Act or any applicable regulations of the department.

As an alternative to the Medical Corporation Act, an Illinois medical practice may be incorporated under the Professional Service Corporation Act.[4] This statute permits one or more individuals, each of whom is licensed in Illinois, who perform the same or related professional services to form a professional service organization. For example, a combination of physicians, podiatrists, and dentists would be able to incorporate under this statute to provide related professional services. Again, the organization must obtain a certificate from the department of registration and education.[5]

Physicians may also form a professional association under the act of that name,[6] as well as a partnership under the Illinois Uniform

---

4. Ill. Rev. Stat. ch. 32, ¶ 415-1, et seq. (1985).
5. Theodore LeBlang and W. Eugene Basanta, *The Law of Medical Practice in Illinois* (Rochester, N.Y.: Lawyer's Co-operative Publishing Co., 1986), pp. 134-35 (hereinafter, LeBlang and Basanta).
6. Ill. Rev. Stat. ch. 106, ¶ 101, et seq. (1985).

Partnership Act.[7] Of course, all partners are liable for torts committed by one partner while engaged in the partnership business. Each partner is liable for partnership debts, as well.

Illinois hospitals are normally organized under either the Business Corporation Act or the General Not for Profit Corporation Act.[8] These laws require incorporators of such medical corporations to sign and file articles of incorporation with the Secretary of State. The articles of incorporation specify the name of the corporation, its purposes, the term of corporate duration, the address of registered office and agent, and, in the case of business corporations, the number, classes, and value of shares or proprietary interests in the corporation.

Virtually all states take very seriously the requirement that such professional corporations or associations must be composed only of licensed professionals. For example, in Morelli v. Eshan,[9] Eshan and Morelli formed a partnership to provide health care. Morelli was a nonphysician who was responsible for the management of the business. The partners had a falling out, and Morelli petitioned for a dissolution so that he could get his share of the partnership's assets. The trial court granted summary judgment for Eshan, because Morelli's participation constituted the unlicensed practice of medicine. Under Washington law, professional corporations may be organized only by licensed professionals. The court of appeals remanded for an accounting of the respective partners' assets, fashioning a good faith exception. The Washington Supreme Court reversed, finding that such an exception violated the deterrent purpose of the law. Thus, the decision denied Morelli any recovery from his investment in the illegal partnership.

❖ Alternative Delivery Systems

The recent growth of alternative delivery systems for healthcare services, such as health maintenance organizations (HMOs) and preferred provider organizations (PPOs), has been accompanied by

---

7. Ill. Rev. Stat. ch. 106½, ¶ 1, et seq. (1985).
8. Ill. Rev. Stat. ch. 32, ¶ 101.01, et seq. (1985).
9. 756 P.2d 129 (Wash., 1988).

state and federal regulation designed to both encourage the formation of such entities to control costs and regulate them to ensure they provide quality health care. An HMO is an entity that provides comprehensive healthcare services to its membership for a fixed, per capita fee. Physicians generally receive a fixed fee or a salary from the HMO rather than reimbursement based on the cost or amount of services performed. A PPO consists of a series of contracts between third-party payers, subscribers, and healthcare providers that encourage subscribers to avoid nonparticipating physicians through various mechanisms, such as, for example, higher deductibles.[10]

State Law

HMOs are regulated by both state and federal law. Most states have HMO enabling acts, which address both the insurance and healthcare delivery issues of HMO structures. A number of states have taken steps to ensure the fiscal soundness of HMOs, typically by requiring restricted reserves, net worth requirements, and strict accounting and reporting standards. Others have established HMO guaranty funds to which HMOs must contribute. In Illinois, for example, under the Health Maintenance Organization Act,[11] the Illinois Department of Insurance reviews the fiscal and financial solvency of HMOs and the Illinois Department of Public Health assesses the quality of care and services provided by HMOs.

In Illinois, an HMO must apply for a certificate of authority to operate in the state. Before the Illinois Department of Insurance grants such a certificate, the Illinois Department of Public Health must certify that

❖ The HMO has demonstrated a willingness and ability to ensure that the healthcare services it proposes to offer will be provided through adequate personnel and facilities.

---

10. *See, generally*, Furrow et al., p. 71; Charles Steele and Mary Huff, "Antitrust Issues Related to Health Maintenance Organizations and Preferred Provider Organizations," *Managed Health Care 1988* (New York: Practicing Law Institute, 1988), pp. 323-28.
11. Ill. Rev. Stat. ch. 111½, ¶ 1401 (1985).

❖ The HMO has arrangements in conformity with pertinent regulations for an ongoing quality of healthcare assurance program.

The Illinois Department of Insurance will then issue a certificate of authority if the following conditions, among others, are met:

❖ The persons responsible for the conduct and affairs of the applicant are competent and trustworthy, and possess good reputations.
❖ The healthcare plan furnishes basic healthcare services, as defined by regulations, on a prepaid basis, through insurance or otherwise, except to the extent of reasonable requirements for copayments.
❖ The HMO is financially responsible and may reasonably be expected to meet its obligations to enrollees and prospective enrollees.

This act provides that the director of the Illinois Department of Insurance may suspend or revoke an HMO's certificate of authority for a number of reasons, such as if it operates in contravention of its basic organization document or its healthcare plan, or in any manner contrary to the information submitted in its application; if it is no longer financially responsible; or if its continued operation would be hazardous to its enrollees. In addition, the Illinois Department of Public Health regulates HMOs by assessing the quality of their care and services.[12]

Although PPOs are not regulated in every state, Illinois regulates PPOs under the Health Care Reimbursement Reform Act of 1985.[13] PPOs must register with the Illinois Department of Insurance and comply with regulations promulgated by the Department.

States typically regulate other healthcare entities as well. Among other healthcare facilities that a state may regulate through specifying organization requirements are

---

12. LeBlang and Basanta, pp. 156-67, and *1992 Cumulative Supplement*, 80-89.
13. Ill. Rev. Stat. ch. 73, ¶ 982f, et seq. (1985).

- ambulatory surgical centers
- chemical dependency care units
- clinical laboratories
- freestanding emergency or ambulatory care centers
- hospice care programs
- home healthcare agencies
- nursing homes
- continuing care retirement centers
- psychiatric care centers

Federal Law

The federal government also regulates HMOs. The Health Maintenance Organization Act of 1973[14] provided for federal recognition of HMOs, thereby—until recently—providing access to federal grants, loans, and loan guarantees. However, to qualify for federal support, HMOs had to offer comprehensive benefits and meet onerous regulations. Obviously, the process of qualifying for Medicare funds subjects HMOs to federal regulation. So far, the federal government has not directly regulated PPOs, although other federal laws, like the antitrust laws, could apply to either HMOs or PPOs.

The long-term care industry is particularly well regulated by both the state and the federal governments, mainly through licensure.

As you can see, merely deciding on and qualifying for a particular form of business enterprise subjects your facility to a great deal of governmental regulation. As the remaining chapters demonstrate, keeping that enterprise functioning requires compliance with many more laws and regulations.

---

14. 42 U.S.C. § 300e, et seq. (1992).

Regulation Through Licensure

A healthcare professional must have a license to practice. Similarly, once a healthcare facility has qualified as a professional corporation or other business entity, it must receive a license to perform its healthcare services. Medical licensing statutes protect the health, safety, and welfare of the community and thus are supported by the police power of the states. Through licensing statutes, the states control entry into the medical profession, both for practitioners and entities, and take disciplinary actions against individual practitioners or entities that violate professional standards.

❖ Licensing of Healthcare Professionals

No one has an absolute constitutional right to practice a profession such as medicine.[1] Rather, it is a privilege. However, because the courts have recognized a property right in the practice of medicine, the state must provide due process in the granting, denial, or removal of the privilege and must not deny or remove the privilege without good cause or do so arbitrarily. The limitations a state places upon the right to practice a profession must bear some rea-

---

1. Bradwell v. Illinois, 16 Wall. 130, 21 L. Ed 442 (1872).

sonable relationship to the qualifications that are necessary to practice that profession.[2]

The goals of physician and other healthcare professional regulation are

- ❖ Protection of the health and safety of the public
- ❖ Protection of the public from economic fraud by a physician
- ❖ Rehabilitation of the substandard practitioner without arbitrarily destroying his or her career and livelihood[3]

State licensure seeks to meet these goals by only granting individuals the right to practice a profession after certifying that they possess a minimum degree of competence. State preconditions to practice have traditionally included academic qualifications, training and experience, passing an examination, and personal qualifications such as moral fitness.[4] California, for example, requires

- ❖ A diploma issued by an approved medical school
- ❖ An official transcript or other official evidence showing each approved medical school in which a resident course of professional instruction was pursued covering the minimum requirements for certification as a physician and surgeon, and that a diploma and degree were granted by the school
- ❖ Such other information concerning the professional instruction and preliminary education of the applicant as the California Division of Licensing may require
- ❖ An affidavit showing to the satisfaction of the division that the applicant is the person named in each diploma and transcript that he or she submits, that he or she is the lawful holder thereof, and that the

---

2. Aaron R. Caruso, "The Time Present Foundation of the Maryland Medical Professional Regulation," *Courts, Health Science & the Law* 1, No. 2 (October 1990), p. 251 (hereinafter, Caruso).
3. Frank P. Grad and Noelia Marti, *Physician's Licensure and Discipline* (Dobbs Ferry, N.Y.: Ocean Publications, 1979), pp. 6-7.
4. LeBlang and Basanta, p. 584.

diploma or transcript was procured in the regular course of professional instruction and examination without fraud or misrepresentation
- Fingerprint cards from the applicant in order to establish the identity of the applicant and to determine whether the applicant has a record of any criminal convictions in this state or in any other jurisdiction, including foreign countries[5]

Each applicant must also present an official transcript or other official evidence to the California Division of Licensing that he or she has completed two years of preprofessional postsecondary education or its equivalent before completing the resident course of professional instruction.[6] The required transcript must show that each applicant for a physician's and surgeon's certificate has successfully completed a medical curriculum extending over a period of at least four academic years, or 32 months of actual instruction, in a medical school or schools located in the United States or Canada approved by the division, or in a medical school or schools located outside the United States or Canada that otherwise meets the requirements of this section. The total number of hours of all courses shall consist of a minimum of 4,000 hours. The curriculum for all applicants shall provide for adequate instruction in the following subjects:

- Alcoholism and other chemical substance dependency, detection, and treatment
- Anatomy, including embryology, histology, and neuroanatomy
- Anesthesia
- Biochemistry
- Child abuse detection and treatment
- Dermatology
- Geriatric medicine

---

5. Cal. Bus. & Prof. Code § 2082 (1992).
6. Cal. Bus. & Prof. Code § 2088 (1992).

- Human sexuality
- Medicine, including pediatrics
- Neurology
- Obstetrics and gynecology
- Ophthalmology
- Otolaryngology
- Pathology, bacteriology, and immunology
- Pharmacology
- Physical medicine
- Physiology
- Preventive medicine, including nutrition
- Psychiatry
- Radiology, including radiation safety
- Surgery, including orthopedic surgery
- Therapeutics
- Tropical medicine
- Urology[7]

Most states also require physicians and other healthcare professionals to renew their licenses periodically and to meet continuing education requirements. States may also take disciplinary actions against licensed practitioners for violations of laws or regulations related to the licensee's practice. Sanctions may include not issuing a license; not renewing a license; revoking a license; or other discipline such as suspension, probation, or limitations on practice. For example, the Court of Appeals of Ohio upheld the State Medical Board of Ohio's order suspending a physician's medical license for a three-year probationary period for prescribing amphetamines for weight control to patients for as long as nine years when such drugs were to be used only as a short-term adjunct to a regimen of weight reduction.[8]

---

7. Cal. Bus. & Prof. Code ¶ 2089 (1992).
8. In the Matter of Donald R. Williams, M.D., 1990 WL 63027 (Ohio Ct. App. 1990).

The law is clear that when a governmental agency, such as a state medical board, takes a disciplinary action involving a practitioner's property right in the practice of his or her profession, it must afford him due process of law.[9]

Most states do not require certification in a particular specialty as a prerequisite to practicing in that field, although national specialty licensing agencies, such as the American Board of Medical Specialties member boards, offer certification to those who have demonstrated competence in a particular field. Such specialty certification is a guide to patients, not a prerequisite to practicing in most states.[10] In addition, many hospital medical staffs consider board certification a prerequisite to staff appointment.

❖ Facility Licensure

State licensure is also the primary means of regulating hospitals and other healthcare facilities. States regulate such entities under licensing statutes and applicable regulations promulgated thereunder. In Texas, for example, a hospital seeking a license must apply to the Texas Department of Health, Health Facility Licensure and Certification Division, on a form provided by the department showing that:

- ❖ At least one physician is on the medical staff of the hospital, including evidence that the physician is currently licensed.
- ❖ The governing body of the hospital has adopted and implemented a patient transfer policy.

The application must be accompanied by a copy of the hospital's current patient transfer policy and a license fee, which shall be refunded to the applicant if the application is denied. The department may require that the application be approved by the local health authority or other local official for compliance with munic-

---

9. *See, for example*, Klein v. Department of Registration & Education, 105 N.E.2d 758 (Ill. 1952).
10. Caruso, p. 252.

ipal ordinances on building construction, fire prevention, and sanitation.[11]

Texas' *Hospital Licensing Standards*[12] consist of 102 single-spaced pages specifying standards in 11 areas:

- ❖ Existing facilities, operational requirements
- ❖ Existing hospitals
- ❖ Renovation projects
- ❖ Application of standards
- ❖ Submittal requirements
- ❖ Hospital site
- ❖ General hospital
- ❖ Mechanical requirements
- ❖ Electrical requirements
- ❖ Codes and standards
- ❖ Rules governing hospital patient transfer policies and agreements

States can certainly deny, suspend, or revoke a facility's license if it fails to comply with the statutes and regulations governing the facility. Of course, the facility has a right to due process—notice and an opportunity to be heard—before the state takes the sanction and usually may appeal an adverse decision by the agency to a court. For example, in Thompson v. Division of Health of Missouri,[13] the court reversed an order suspending a nursing home license because the Division of Health of Missouri had not complied with a requirement to reinspect the facility to see whether the deficiencies—poor medical charting, lack of employee health records, and deficiencies in staffing schedules—had been corrected before suspending the facility.

Because license revocation may disrupt the lives and health of patients/residents and may aggravate a shortage of beds, state

---

11. Tex. Health & Safety Code § 241.022 (1991).
12. Texas Department of Health, Health Facility Licensure and Certification Division, *Hospital Licensing Standards* (1985) (amended through June 1, 1991).
13. 604 S.W. 2d 802 (Mo. Ct. App. 1980).

healthcare agencies often try so-called intermediate sanctions. Intermediate sanctions include

- ❖ Civil fines.
- ❖ Receivership. In a receivership, the provider retains ownership of the facility, but a court-appointed receiver controls and manages it.
- ❖ Suspension of admissions.
- ❖ Public monitors. This sanction allows a state agency to appoint a person to be present in a facility to monitor its performance.

All states permit their health departments or similar licensing agencies to inspect and require reports from facilities subject to licensure.

The federal government is more indirectly involved in facility licensure than are the states, but by specifying conditions states must comply with to receive federal funds, the federal agencies indirectly "write" state regulations. For example, the Medicaid laws require that state plans for medical assistance include standards for institutions treating Medicaid recipients. The federal government does not "license" nonfederal hospitals, but "certifying" them to receive payments under Medicare or Medicaid is in practice very similar to state licensure. In order to receive payments under Medicare or Medicaid, an institutional provider must be certified and sign a provider agreement. A hospital, for example, meets the Medicare conditions of participation if it is accredited by the Joint Commission on the Accreditation of Healthcare Organizations (JCAHO), unless a Medicare inspection indicates noncompliance.[14] Medicare requires providers receiving Medicare payments to meet standards concerning the screening, treatment, and discharge of patients, including patients who are not Medicare patients, who come to the facility's emergency room.

---

14. 42 U.S.C. §§ 1395x(e)-1395bb (1992).

❖ Certificates of Need

In many states, obtaining a license is not enough to open a new facility or even to purchase a new piece of expensive medical equipment. Because of the theory summarized in chapter 1, that hospitals seek to recruit physicians, not patients, often by purchasing new and expensive medical technology, thus creating an imbalance in supply and demand, most states require certificates of need (CON), which require healthcare facilities to demonstrate a need to expand or to acquire the new equipment as a prerequisite to obtaining the government's approval for the acquisition. Illinois, for example, requires a CON in the following circumstances:

- ❖ the establishment or discontinuation of a healthcare facility
- ❖ a substantial change in the bed capacity of a healthcare facility
- ❖ the establishment or discontinuation of a category of service by a healthcare facility
- ❖ any capital expenditure that exceeds the capital expenditure minimum ($1 million for major medical equipment and $2 million for all other capital expenditures, subject to annual inflation adjustments)
- ❖ the acquisition of major medical equipment that exceeds the capital expenditure limit[15]

Illinois considers the following factors in determining whether to grant a CON:

- ❖ whether the applicant is fit, willing, and able to provide a proper standard of health care to the community
- ❖ whether economic feasibility is demonstrated in terms of effect on the existing and projected operating budget of the applicant and of the healthcare facility,

---

15. Ill. Rev. Stat. ch. 111½, ¶ 1153 (1985).

including the applicant's ability to satisfy pertinent state licensure regulations, and the projected impact on the total healthcare expenditures in the facility and community

- whether the applicant's purpose in requesting a CON is consistent with the public interest
- whether the proposed project is consistent with the orderly and economic development of such facilities and equipment and is in accord with the standards, criteria, or healthcare facility plans adopted by the Illinois Health Facilities Planning Board[16]

An applicant who is denied a CON typically has a right to a hearing before the state agency and may seek judicial review of an adverse decision.

Congress repealed the federal version of the CON program in 1986.[17]

States typically ascertain the appropriate level of demand for health services and then determine what amount of health resource is needed to satisfy that demand. Then they allocate the permitted level of health resource supply among the facilities.[18]

No doubt exists that modern licensing standards are becoming more and more detailed and pervasive. The technological revolution in health care has led to regulation of new technologies. As facilities added renal dialysis units, kidney transplant units, cardiac catheterization laboratories, and the like, states created a system of licensure within licensure, requiring a facility that wants to offer a special service to obtain a special permit in addition to its regular license and to comply with new regulations governing the standards for operating such a service.[19] These pervasive licensing requirements are not without their critics, however:

---

16. *Id.* ¶ 1156; 77 Ill. Admin. Code §§ 1100, et seq.
17. P.L. No. 99-660, § 701(a), 100 Stat. 3743, 3799 (1986).
18. Furrow et al., pp. 682-84.
19. Louise Sander, "Licensing of Health Care Facilities," in Ruth Roemer and George McKray, eds., *Legal Aspects of Health Policy, Issues and Trends* (Westport, Conn.: Greenwood, 1980), p. 139.

> The trend seems to be moving in the direction of having the state licensing bodies provide a comprehensive definition of the specific components, e.g., departmental structures, numbers of beds, occupancy rate, services provided, number and qualifications of staff, etc., which must be present within the various levels of healthcare facilities as well as within each of their departments. For the administration and board of trustees, the decision-making sphere seems to be circumscribed to the point of deciding whether or not to conform to the regulations rather than to decide on the optimal mix of personnel and resources to provide acceptable and efficient care.[20]

Because these pervasive licensing regulations are not about to go away, the challenge for the healthcare financial manager is to find a way to comply with them in a cost-effective way so as not to subject his or her facility to the financial and other losses associated with a license revocation, suspension, or other sanction.

---

20. Kathleen M. Popko, *Regulatory Controls: Implications for the Community Hospital* (Lexington, Mass.: Lexington Books 1976), p. 45.

Private Regulation

Even though governments regulate healthcare facilities through statutes and regulations detailing the requirements for corporate status and licensing, in many respects they defer to accreditation by private organizations, particularly the Joint Commission on the Accreditation of Healthcare Organizations (JCAHO), the leading healthcare facility accreditation organization. The JCAHO and other private, voluntary accreditation organizations represent a classic form of self-regulation. The professionals and institutions participating in such organizations' programs establish quality standards and inspect participating facilities to determine whether they meet the standards.

❖ The Joint Commission on the Accreditation of Healthcare Organizations

The JCAHO is a private, not-for-profit association that is the successor to the American College of Surgeons Hospital Standardization Program, established in 1919. Its purpose is to improve the quality of care and services provided in healthcare settings through a voluntary accreditation process. The governing and policy-making members of the JCAHO compose a board of commissioners. The board of commissioners, in turn, comprises individuals from the American Hospital Association (AHA), the American Medical Association (AMA), the American College of Physicians, the American College of Surgeons, and the American Dental Association.[1]

The JCAHO formulates and annually updates accreditation standards.[2] JCAHO accreditation standards are a useful guide for hospitals. Hospitals that seek accreditation from JCAHO must apply, pay a fee, and participate in an intensive survey to determine whether the institution is able to satisfy the standards established by the JCAHO and published in its *Accreditation Manual for Hospitals*.[3] JCAHO also surveys hospitals to measure and encourage compliance with accreditation standards. Hospitals that substantially comply[4] with JCAHO standards are accredited by the JCAHO for three years.

Further, several states currently accept JCAHO accreditation as a basis for either full or partial licensure without a separate inspection by the state.[5] In Alabama, for example, all hospitals accredited by the JCAHO shall be deemed by the state health department to be licensable without further inspection or survey by the Alabama State Department of Health, although the statute notes that such accreditation does not relieve that hospital of the responsibility of applying for licensure and remitting the appropriate licensure fee.[6]

Other states use JCAHO inspections as a substitute for inspecting themselves. In Alaska, for example, the Alaska Department of Health and Social Services may accept accreditation by the JCAHO in lieu of an annual inspection by the department for the year in which the accreditation was granted if the accreditation standards of the commission are substantially similar to the inspection standards of the department.[7]

In addition, JCAHO accreditation is a prerequisite for payment by some health insurance plans and is required in practice for a

---

1. LeBlang and Basanta, p. 315.
2. *Id.*, pp. 315-316.
3. Miller, pp. 45-46.
4. Joint Commission on the Accreditation of Healthcare Organizations, *Accreditation Manual for Hospitals, 1991,* xi (Chicago: JCAHO, 1991). Substantial compliance is met when a hospital consistently meets all the major provisions of the standard. *Id.* at ix.
5. Miller, p. 46.
6. Ala. Code § 22-21-24 (1991).
7. Alaska Stat. § 18.20.080 (1991).

hospital to be approved for a residency program.[8] Similarly, Medicare law and regulations[9] state that hospitals accredited by JCAHO meet most of the conditions for Medicare certification, unless an inspection by Medicare inspectors discovers that the institution is not in compliance.[10] Given the importance of receiving JCAHO accreditation, it is not surprising that over 80 percent of acute care hospitals and virtually all hospitals with more than 25 beds are JCAHO accredited.[11]

JCAHO accreditation is also relied on heavily by the private healthcare sector. For example, such accreditation is a requirement for participation in some medical insurance plans, and some professional organizations limit membership to professionals associated with accredited facilities.[12]

The JCAHO accredits seven categories of service:

- acute care hospitals
- long-term care organizations
- nonhospital based psychiatric and substance abuse organizations, including community mental health centers and services for persons with mental retardation or other developmental disabilities
- ambulatory healthcare organizations
- managed care organizations
- hospice programs
- home care organizations[13]

When a hospital applies for accreditation, it is surveyed by the JCAHO team based on the category or categories of services provided. After an on-site survey, the surveyors meet with various

---

8. Furrow et al., p. 100.
9. 42 U.S.C.A. § 1395x(c), 1395bb (1992).
10. Miller, p. 46.
11. *Id.*
12. Timothy S. Jost, "The Joint Commission on the Accreditation of Hospitals: Private Regulation of Health Care and the Public Interest," *Boston College Law Review* XXIV, No. 4 (July 1983), pp. 835, 845.
13. Joint Commission on Accreditation of Healthcare Organizations, *Accreditation Manual for Hospitals, 1991,* xviii (Chicago: JCAHO, 1990).

representatives of the hospital.[14] Recommendations are then made by the surveyors to the JCAHO staff. The JCAHO staff, in turn, makes recommendations to the JCAHO Accreditation Committee for action.[15] A hospital can institute appellate procedures if the Accreditation Committee denies accreditation.[16]

Some areas to which the JCAHO Accreditation Standards and Licensing Requirements apply are[17]

- admission
- anesthesia services
- dietetic services
- discharge
- emergency care and services
- home care services
- hospital-sponsored ambulatory care services
- infection control
- medical record services and hospital records
- nuclear medicine services
- pathology and medical laboratory services
- patients' rights and responsibilities
- pharmaceutical services
- plant, technology, and safety management
- professional library services
- quality assurance
- radiology services
- rehabilitation and restorative services
- respiratory care services
- social work services

---

14. Joint Commission on Accreditation of Healthcare Organizations, *Accreditation Manual for Hospitals, 1991*, xx and xxi (Chicago: JCAHO, 1990).
15. Joint Commission on Accreditation of Healthcare Organizations, *Accreditation Manual for Hospitals, 1991*, xxv (Chicago: JCAHO, 1990).
16. *Id.*
17. Joint Commission on Accreditation of Healthcare Organizations, *Accreditation Manual for Hospitals, 1991* (Chicago: JCAHO, 1990); LeBlang and Basanta, pp. 315-60.

- special care units
- surgical and recovery room services
- utilization review

For example, in Illinois, to meet the requirements of a standardized quality assurance program, hospitals must have a program that consistently monitors and evaluates the quality of patient care.[18] The hospital governing board and the medical staff must work together to develop and implement the quality assurance program. This program must include the following[19]:

- The medical staff must monitor and evaluate the quality and appropriateness of patient care as well as the clinical performance of all individuals with staff privileges through monthly meetings of clinical departments, surgical case review, review of the pharmacy and therapeutics function, drug usage evaluation, medical records review, and blood usage review.
- The quality and appropriateness of patient care in the various hospital services must be monitored and evaluated.
- Hospitals must ensure that the following functions are performed: infection control; utilization review; and review of accidents, injuries, and safety hazards.
- Mechanisms must be implemented for monitoring and evaluating the clinical performance of those individuals who are not permitted to practice independently by the hospital.
- Relevant quality assurance findings must be considered in the reappointment/reappraisal of medical staff members, in the renewal or revision of clinical

---

18. Joint Commission on Accreditation of Healthcare Organizations, *Accreditation Manual for Hospitals, 1991*, Standard QA.1 (Chicago: JCAHO, 1990).
19. Joint Commission on Accreditation of Healthcare Organizations, *Accreditation Manual for Hospitals, 1991*, Standards QA.2, QA.2.1, QA.2.2, QA.2.3, QA.2.4, and QA.2.5 (Chicago: JCAHO, 1990).

privileges of individuals who practice independently, and in the appraisal of those practitioners who are not permitted by the hospital to practice independently.

JCAHO standards may play an important role in malpractice litigation. For example, in Darling v. Charleston Community Memorial Hospital,[20] the court upheld a jury verdict against a hospital for failing to review the operative procedures of one of its emergency room physicians; to exercise adequate supervision over the case; and to require consultation, particularly after complications had developed. The court relied on the JCAHO standards in finding that the hospital had a duty to supervise the physician and the case. Failure to follow the JCAHO standards created a permissive inference of negligence on the part of the hospital that the jury could accept or reject.

❖ Other Private Regulatory Organizations

Many private organizations involved with health care exist. Common examples are the American Medical Association (AMA), American Hospital Association (AHA), American Osteopathic Association (AOA), and, of course, the Healthcare Financial Management Association (HFMA). Like the JCAHO, these organizations at least indirectly regulate healthcare providers in two ways: by promulgating position papers on various aspects of health care that, like the JCAHO standards, can provide evidence of the proper level of care, and also by influencing the passage of legislation and the promulgation of regulations that directly regulate health care. For example, the Council on Medical Education of the AMA approves hospital internship and residency programs, and the American College of Surgeons approves cancer therapy programs.[21]

In addition, physician specialty board certification and various allied medical professionals indirectly regulate the industry by set-

---

20. 211 N.E.2d 253 (Ill. 1965), *cert. denied* 383 U.S. 946 (1966).
21. Ruth Roemer, "Regulation of Health Personnel," in Ruth Roemer and George McKray, eds., *Legal Aspects of Health Policy, Issues and Trends* (Westport, Conn.: Greenwood, 1980), p. 101.

ting qualifications for certification as specialists. Even though certification as a specialist is not a prerequisite for licensure, many facilities require board certification for staff appointments, especially because many federal or state reimbursement programs limit payment to board-certified specialists or set differential rates for them.

Another important form of private regulation consists of clinical practice protocols or practice parameters developed by specialty societies such as the American Academy of Pediatrics. Such clinical standards regulate professional services by being presumptive evidence of the due care required to avoid malpractice liability. In fact, one state has passed a law immunizing physicians from a malpractice lawsuit if they practiced in accordance with such medical practice guidelines.[22]

In addition, state medical societies and associations play a prominent role in disciplining physicians in many states.

Thus, JCAHO and many other private, voluntary accreditation organizations represent a classic form of self-regulation.[23] The professionals and institutions that participate in these programs establish the standards of quality health care.[24]

---

22. Furrow et al., pp. 139-40. *See* Maine General Laws, Ch. 931 (1990).
23. Furrow et al., p. 100.
24. *Id.*

6

Self-Regulation

Even if healthcare providers did not have the pervasive governmental and private regulation discussed in the previous chapters, they would still regulate themselves so as to provide quality health care in an efficient manner. Although some critics of healthcare regulation contend that self-regulation consists of little more than deciding whether to follow the statutes, regulations, and Joint Commission on the Accreditation of Healthcare Organizations (JCAHO) and other standards, in today's complex healthcare environment, self-regulation under the facility's articles of incorporation and bylaws and by the facility's governing board, administrators, and medical staff is as important as ever.

❖ Articles of Incorporation and Bylaws

Under state law, to form a corporation, either for-profit or not-for-profit, a healthcare entity must file articles of incorporation with the secretary of state (see chapter 3). State statutes typically specify the content of articles of incorporation. Typically, articles of incorporation must contain the name of the corporation, its purpose, the name and address of the corporation's registered agent and registered office, and the names of the incorporators. The incorporators will elect the initial board of directors. Thereafter, shareholders of for-profit corporations or members of not-for-profit ones will elect the board of directors in accordance with the provisions set out in the bylaws.

Bylaws are rules for the government of a corporation. Shareholders or members have the inherent power to draft bylaws but often delegate that power to the directors. They may contain any internal operating rules that are not illegal or inconsistent with the articles of incorporation. In Utah, for example, the articles or the bylaws of health facilities must specify

- the duties and responsibilities of the board (governing body)
- the method for election or appointment to the board
- the size of the board
- the terms of office of the board
- the methods for removal of board members and officers
- the duties and responsibilities of the officers and any standing committees
- to whom responsibility for operation and maintenance of the hospital, including evaluation of hospital practices, may be delegated
- the methods established by the board for holding such individuals responsible
- the mechanism for formal approval of the organization, bylaws, rules of the medical staff and hospital departments
- the frequency of meetings[1]

In addition, the medical staff must have bylaws that are adopted by the governing board. The JCAHO specifies that in order to establish a framework for self-governance and to separate its duties and responsibilities from those of the hospital, the medical staff should develop bylaws, rules, and regulations that are adopted by

---

1. Utah Admin. R. 432-100-4.102 (1990).

the hospital governing board.[2] Utah's medical staff bylaws, for example, must contain provisions detailing the credentialing process (the process of approving a healthcare professional's access to healthcare facilities—the granting of hospital privileges), including:

- the necessary qualifications for medical staff membership
- the delineation of privileges
- the scope of privileges for specified professionals who are not members of the medical staff
- a provision that the members of the medical staff must be legally, professionally, and ethically qualified
- a requirement that the medical care of all persons admitted to the hospital shall be under the supervision and direction of a fully qualified physician who is licensed by the state
- a prohibition against denying an applicant for medical staff membership and/or privileges solely on the ground that the applicant is a licensed podiatrist rather than licensed to practice medicine
- a prohibition against denying membership and/or privileges on any ground prohibited by law[3]

❖ The Governing Board

The hospital governing board makes the major decisions of the hospital. The board is responsible for the conduct of the hospital's operations, including allocating resources and overseeing the quality of medical care.[4] The board develops policy, plans for institu-

---

2. Joint Commission on the Accreditation of Healthcare Organizations, *Accreditation Manual for Hospitals, 1991* Standard M.S.2 (Chicago: JCAHO, 1990).
3. Utah Admin. R. 432-100-4.302 (1990).
4. American Medical Association and American Hospital Association, *The Report of the Joint Task Force on Hospital-Medical Staff Relationships* 9 (Chicago: AMA and AHA, 1985).

tional goals, and controls the performance of both the lay and the professional staffs of the facility.[5]

The Texas Department of Health's *Hospital Licensing Standards*, for example, requires that for each hospital there shall be a governing authority (the board), responsible for its organization, management, control, and operation, including appointment of the medical staff. The standards add that

- ❖ The board shall be formally organized in accordance with a written constitution and bylaws that must clearly set forth organization, duties, responsibilities, and relationships.
- ❖ The board must meet regularly and keep written records of its meetings.
- ❖ The board shall appoint a competent executive officer or administrator and vest that person with authority and responsibility for carrying out its policies.
- ❖ The governing board shall give the necessary authority to the administrator for the administration of the hospital in all its activities and departments, subject only to such policies as may be adopted and such orders as may be issued by the governing board in accordance with its bylaws.
- ❖ The governing board shall employ or authorize the administrator to employ personnel to carry out the functions of the hospital as specified in the standards.
- ❖ The governing board shall appoint members of the medical staff under a formal procedure established in both hospital and medical staff bylaws.
- ❖ The board is responsible for the maintenance of proper standards of professional work in the hospital and shall require that the medical staff function in conformity with reasonable standards of competency.[6]

---

5. Joint Commission on the Accreditation of Healthcare Organizations, *Accreditation Manual for Hospitals, 1991* Standards GB.1 to GB.3 (1980). *See, generally*, LeBlang and Basanta, pp. 306-8.
6. Texas Department of Health, Health Facility Licensure and Certification Division, *Hospital Licensing Standards* 1-6.1 (1985) (amended through June 1, 1991).

Board members—trustees—are fiduciaries. A fiduciary is one who holds a position of trust or confidence and who must be both loyal and responsible. A trustee's fiduciary duty of loyalty requires that he or she place the interests of the facility above personal interests. Thus, a trustee cannot, for example, compete with the hospital or profit by his or her position other than by the receipt of duly authorized compensation for services. The fiduciary duty of responsibility requires that the trustee use reasonable care, skill, and diligence in performing his or her duties. The law defines *reasonable care* as that care that an ordinary, prudent trustee would use under the same or similar circumstances. Although a trustee may get help in carrying out duties, he or she is personally responsible for fulfilling them. A trustee could, for example, ask for and receive a report from medical professionals concerning the credentials and abilities of a prospective member of the medical staff but could not, however, delegate his or her vote on the appointment of that physician to the medical staff. Further, the trustee would have an obligation to ensure the quality of the information on which his or her decision was based.

If a trustee fails to perform his or her fiduciary duties properly—if the trustee fails to use reasonable care, skill, and diligence in performing them—a court can find him or her liable for the consequences of this failure to perform. For example, the California attorney general successfully sued the trustees of a charitable corporation for lost interest incurred because of the trustees' negligence in failing to transfer surplus funds to an interest-bearing account.[7] Of course, a trustee is liable only for his or her own negligence. A court would not, for example, find a trustee liable for medical malpractice if a staff physician were negligent during surgery, at least as long as the trustee had properly fulfilled the responsibilities of ensuring that the physician had the proper credentials and skill for his or her appointment to the staff.

❖ The Facility Administrator

The hospital administrator is the chief executive officer of the facility. The governing board appoints the administrator and vests

---

7. Lynch v. Redfield Foundation, 9 Cal. App. 3d 293 (1970).

him or her with the authority necessary to carry out the board's policies. JCAHO standards require the administrator to be qualified by education and expertise sufficient to fulfill his or her assigned responsibilities.[8]

The hospital administrator is responsible for implementing the policies and accomplishing the goals of the trustees. Specifically, the administrator

- organizes the administrative functions
- establishes accountabilities
- facilitates effective communication between the medical staff and the facility's departments
- organizes the facility's internal structure
- manages the facility's finances
- provides for the appropriate use of the physical resources of the facility[9]

In addition, the administrator is responsible for day-to-day communication with the medical staff and serves as the primary liaison between the medical staff and the governing board.[10]

❖ The Medical Staff

The medical staff plays an important role in the self-regulation of any healthcare facility. The medical staff is an organized body composed of individuals whom the governing board has authorized to practice their profession in the facility within the scope of their delineated clinical privileges. *Clinical privileges* are the permission or authority to provide medical or other patient care services in the institution within specified limits. The medical staff has overall responsibility for the quality of professional services and is ac-

---

8. Joint Commission on the Accreditation of Healthcare Organizations, *Accreditation Manual for Hospitals, 1991* Standard MA.1.1 (Chicago: JCAHO, 1990).
9. *Id.*, Standards MA.1.2-MA.1.7.
10. LeBlang and Basanta, p. 308.

countable to the governing body. JCAHO also requires the medical staff bylaws and rules and regulations to describe the process the facility is to follow when delineating privileges.

Many hospitals have several categories of medical staff membership:

- active staff
- associate staff—members being considered for advancement to the active medical staff
- consulting staff—highly qualified practitioners who are available as consultants when needed
- courtesy staff—those who have the privilege to admit an occasional patient to the facility
- honorary staff—former members honored with emeritus positions or other outstanding practitioners whom the medical staff desires to honor[11]

Physicians on a hospital medical staff function on two levels. The medical staff has overall responsibility for the quality of physician services within the hospital. Thus, on this level, the individual physician functions as part of a collective group that monitors patient care. On another level, the practitioner is an individual provider of healthcare services.[12]

Healthcare facility trustees make the formal grant of hospital staff privileges to practitioners, either themselves or by adopting bylaws delegating the decision making to a committee, such as a credentials committee. Because many healthcare trustees are nonphysicians, they must rely heavily on staff physicians composing such peer review groups. These groups carry out the credentialing and peer review functions to fulfill the trustees' duty of ensuring that patients receive quality medical care and are not harmed by the misconduct or incompetence of a practitioner. Although the governing board takes ultimate responsibility for failures in the

---

11. Edna Huffman, *Medical Record Management*, 9th ed. (Berwyn, Ill.: Physician's Record Co., 1990), pp. 20-21.
12. Karen Steimetz, "Medical Staff Membership Decisions: Judicial Intervention," *University of Illinois Law Review* (1985) p. 473.

quality of care its facility provides, only physicians, and often only specialists in the applicant's specialty, can undertake the technical review of the qualifications and practice required.

Determining who will be allowed to practice medicine in the facility is obviously an important internal regulation. Just because a physician or other professional has a license does not make that practitioner competent. Courts have recently begun to hold facilities liable for the malpractice of a physician who should not have been appointed to the medical staff or who should have his or her privileges limited. For example, in Jane Doe v. Victory Memorial Hospital, et al.,[13] a patient suffered complications after an elective hysterectomy conducted by a recently hired surgeon who had just completed his residency. The patient sued the hospital. She contended that although the hospital had obtained a list of the number and types of prior surgeries in which the surgeon had participated and had asked for and received his prior hospital's endorsement, the hospital was negligent not to have inquired into his competence in specific surgical procedures, especially because Victory Memorial granted him virtually unlimited privileges. Under Victory's privileges, he could perform surgeries that were not even performed at the hospital in which he took his residency. Nor did the facility supervise his work. The jury agreed that this was negligent and found the hospital liable for 45 percent of the total damages.

The credentials committee evaluates the credentials of each applicant for medical staff privileges and recommends whether the facility should grant privileges. The credentials committee also sets the parameters of the clinical privileges of members of the medical staff and investigates charges of poor performance and violations of hospital or other rules.[14]

In addition to the credentials committee, many facilities have the medical specialty department of the applicant's specialty review the application before it goes to the credentials committee. The credentials committee also reviews the application and makes a

---

13. No. 86 CV 107 (Chippewa Co., Wisconsin, reported November 30, 1987), discussed in Frank Woodside and Nancy Cody, "Physician's Advocate," *Legal Aspects of Medical Practice* 16, No. 1 (January 1988), p. 4.
14. Christopher Morter, "The Health Care Quality Improvement Act of 1986: Will Physicians Find Peer Review More Inviting?" *Virginia Law Review* 74 (September 1988), p. 1115.

recommendation to the executive committee of the medical staff for action, although in some facilities the entire medical staff votes. Based on the reports of the clinical departments, the credentials committee, and any others that may have been involved, the executive committee recommends denial, reduction, or revocation of privileges. The governing board has the final decision-making authority over medical staff appointments although, as a practical matter, it is likely to defer to the medical staff's judgment.[15]

Quality assurance—the evaluation of the quality and appropriateness of patient care—is an important internal regulation of health care carried out by the medical staff. The Joint Commission on the Accreditation of Healthcare Organizations and most states require hospitals to have an ongoing quality assurance program.[16] Illinois, for example, requires the governing board and the medical staff to have a program of quality assurance that includes these features:

- The medical staff must monitor and evaluate the quality and appropriateness of patient care as well as the clinical performance of all individuals with staff privileges through monthly meetings of clinical departments, surgical case review, review of the pharmacy and therapeutics function, drug usage evaluation, medical records review, and blood usage review.
- The facility must evaluate the quality and appropriateness of patient care in the various hospital services.
- Hospitals must ensure that the following functions are performed: infection control; utilization review; and review of accidents, injuries, and safety hazards.
- The hospital must implement mechanisms for monitoring and evaluating the clinical performance of those individuals who are not permitted to practice independently by the hospital.

---

15. Karen Steimetz, "Medical Staff Membership Decisions: Judicial Intervention," *University of Illinois Law Review* (1985), p. 473.
16. Joint Commission on the Accreditation of Healthcare Organizations, *Accreditation Manual for Hospitals, 1992*, Standard QA.1 (Chicago: JCAHO, 1991).

❖ The facility must consider relevant quality assurance findings in the reappointment/reappraisal of medical staff members, the renewal or revision of clinical privileges of individuals who practice independently, and in the appraisal of those practitioners who are not permitted by the hospital to practice independently.[17]

Peer review groups use medical review criteria to review the appropriateness of medical or surgical procedures. The Institute of Medicine committee of the National Academy of Science defines medical review criteria as "systematically developed statements that can be used to assess the appropriateness of specific healthcare decisions, services, and outcomes."[18] Obviously, such internal review is an important internal regulation mechanism to ensure quality patient care.

Financial managers should familiarize themselves with the facility's articles of incorporation and bylaws, as well as understanding the roles and responsibilities of the governing board, the facility administrator, and the medical staff, and how they interact, to help the facility's self-regulation lower the costs of complying with external regulation.

---

17. *Id. See, generally,* LeBlang and Basanta, pp. 348-49.
18. Shirley Kellie and John Kelley, "Medicare Peer Review Organization Preprocedure Review Criteria: An Analysis of Criteria for Three Procedures," *Journal of the American Medical Association* 265 (March 13, 1991), pp. 1265-70.

Judicial Regulation of the Healthcare Industry

Chapter 2 discussed the role of two of the three branches of government in the regulation of health care. As we have seen, the legislature regulates the healthcare industry by enacting statutes and the executive does likewise through regulations and adjudications by its administrative agencies. We may not think of the third branch—the courts—as "regulating" health care, but they do, in at least two ways: by interpreting statutes and regulations and by establishing precedents in cases involving healthcare facilities.

❖ An Overview of the Judicial System

The states and the federal government have different judicial systems but have some elements in common. All judicial systems have two basic types of courts: trial courts and appellate courts. *Trial courts* initially "hear" a case. A judge or a jury will decide a dispute between two or more parties based on evidence presented by the various parties. *Appellate courts* do not hear evidence but rather decide appeals from the trial court on the basis of the record of the trial.

State Courts

Although each state judicial system is at least a little different from the others, a "generic" state court system is composed of two types of trial courts and several levels of appellate court.

Every state has inferior trial courts of limited jurisdiction. *Jurisdiction* is nothing more than the power to hear and decide a case. Typically, inferior courts' (municipal or city court, for example) jurisdiction is limited to civil suits involving small amounts of money and to minor criminal violations.

States also have trial *courts of general jurisdiction* that can try all kinds of cases, without monetary or subject matter limitation. Most major healthcare cases would be tried in trial courts of general jurisdiction (or in federal court, as described later). Sometimes courts of general jurisdiction also act as appellate courts, hearing appeals from the judgments of inferior trial courts and reviewing the actions of administrative agencies, such as a state licensing authority. For example, in *In re Guess*,[1] after the North Carolina Medical Board revoked Dr. Guess' license based on findings that his practice of homeopathy (a system of therapy based on the theory that large doses of a certain drug given to a healthy person will produce certain conditions that, when occurring spontaneously as symptoms of a disease, are relieved by the same drug in small doses[2]) departed from the standards of acceptable medical practice in the state. Dr. Guess appealed to the Superior Court, which found the board's decision was not based on competent, material, and substantial evidence and was arbitrary and capricious.

Every state has appellate courts, including a "court of last resort," the appellate court at the top of the state's judicial system. Such a court is often called the *state supreme court* but may be called by another name, such as *supreme judicial court,* or even, as in New York, *court of appeals.* Intermediate appellate courts initially hear appeals from the trial courts, and the parties may seek further review in the state supreme court.

As previously noted, an appellate court does not retry the case on its merits—it does not rehear the evidence. Nor will an appellate

---

1. 393 S.E.2d 833 (N.C. 1990).
2. Thomas L. Stedman, *Stedman's Medical Dictionary,* 24th ed. (Baltimore: Williams & Wilkins, 1982), p. 654.

court substitute its ideas of justice for those of the trial court.[3] Rather, the appellate court reviews the record of the case in the trial court to determine whether the trial court committed a procedural error or misapplied the law to the facts of the case, as by giving an improper jury instruction. In the Guess case, the intermediate appellate court, the court of appeals, affirmed the superior court's order reversing the board's decision. The board appealed to the Supreme Court of North Carolina, which reversed the decision of the court of appeals. The Supreme Court of North Carolina found that the court of appeals had erred in interpreting the relevant statute by adding a requirement that the medical practice prohibited by the statute must pose an actual threat of harm to patients. The higher court analyzed the legislative intent in enacting the statute. The court concluded that a general risk of endangering the public is inherent in any practices that do not conform to the standards of acceptable and prevailing medical practice in the state and that the legislature had intended to prohibit any such practice without regard to whether the practice itself could be shown to endanger the public.

The Federal Courts

The basic federal court system consists of trial courts of general jurisdiction, the *federal district courts*; intermediate appellate courts, the *courts of appeals*; and the *U.S. Supreme Court*.

Although federal district courts are similar to state trial courts of general jurisdiction, in one sense the jurisdiction of the federal district courts is limited. They cannot hear cases that fall outside the "judicial power of the United States" as defined in Article III, Section 2, of the U.S. Constitution. Most of the cases heard in the federal courts fall within one of three of the categories of federal jurisdiction:

- ❖ Cases in which the United States is a party, including both civil cases in which the United States is a plaintiff

---

3. *See, generally*, Harry W. Jones, John M. Kernochan, and Arthur W. Murphy, *Legal Method: Cases and Text Materials* (Mineola, N.Y.: The Foundation Press, 1980), pp. 37-42.

or defendant and all prosecutions for violating federal criminal statutes.

❖ Cases involving a federal question—*that is*, the interpretation or effect of the U.S. Constitution or a federal statute or regulation.

❖ Cases involving diversity of citizenship—suits between citizens of different states where the amount involved is greater than $50,000. A healthcare facility would be a citizen of the state in which it is incorporated and of the state in which it has its principal place of business for diversity purposes.

Each state has at least one district court; many states have several. A number of district courts will be under the jurisdiction of the intermediate appellate court, the court of appeals for their particular circuit. A circuit court of appeals will hear appeals from district courts in its circuit. Circuits vary from as small an area as the District of Columbia to the Ninth Circuit, which includes most of the far west, Alaska, and Hawaii.[4]

The U.S. Supreme Court can hear both state and federal appeals that fall within its jurisdiction. For example, the Supreme Court could hear an appeal in a case in which a state supreme court has upheld the validity of a state statute or court decision against a challenge that it violated the U.S. Constitution. For example, in Cruzan v. Director, Missouri Department of Health,[5] the Supreme Court considered whether the Supreme Court of Missouri's decision that because there was no clear and convincing evidence of Nancy Cruzan's desire to have life-sustaining treatment withdrawn when an automobile accident left her in a persistent vegetative state, her parents could not effectuate a request directing the withdrawal of life-sustaining treatment violated the U.S. Constitution. The Court held that the Supreme Court of Missouri's decision did not violate the federal constitution because of the state's interests in protecting human life and guarding personal choice.

---

4. *Id.*, pp. 41-48.
5. 492 U.S. 261 (1990).

❖ Malpractice Litigation

Obviously, one of the major ways in which the courts regulate health care in today's healthcare environment is through malpractice litigation. Ever since 1794, Americans have been suing physicians for medical malpractice.[6] The magnitude of the recent increase in malpractice litigation is illustrated by the fact that 80 percent of the malpractice suits filed between 1935 and 1975 were filed in the last 5 years of that 40-year period.[7]

Courts regulate the provision of health care by setting the standard of care, by deciding who bears the burden of proof, by deciding what evidence is admissible, and by deciding what healthcare providers may be liable, among others.

A physician is liable for malpractice if he or she had a duty to use due care, failed to use such care (that is, was negligent), and the failure resulted in harm to the patient. In medical malpractice cases, the courts determine negligence by measuring the conduct of the defendant physician against the standard of care of the reasonably careful and prudent medical practitioner.[8] In addition, a plaintiff may bring a malpractice suit using a contract theory under which the malpractice is a breach of an express or implied contract to use the requisite degree of skill and care in return for payment of the fee.

The courts have recently made striking changes in the "regulation" of health care by changing the legal doctrines involved in medical malpractice. They have changed the standard of care in many cases from a "local" standard to a "national" one. Until fairly recently, in determining the standard of care, courts were guided by the practice of reasonably well-qualified physicians in the locality in which the defendant physician practices or in similar localities. Recently, however, courts have repudiated the locality rule in favor of a national standard.[9] For example, in Hall v. Hilbun,[10] the Supreme Court of Mississippi, in adopting a national standard, noted:

---

6. Cross v. Guthery, 1 Am. Dec. 61 (1794).
7. Furrow et al., p. 379.
8. LeBlang and Basanta, p. 401.
9. *Id.*, pp. 416-17.
10. 466 So.2d 856 (Miss. 1985).

> We would have to put our heads in the sand to ignore the "nationalization of medical education and training.". . . Nationally uniform standards are enforced in the case of certification of specialists. Differences and changes in these areas occur temporally, not geographically.
>
> Physicians are far more mobile than they once were. They frequently attend medical school in one state, do a residency in another, establish a practice in a third, and after a period of time relocate to a fourth. All the while, they have ready access to professional and scientific journals and seminars for continuing medical education from across the country. Common sense and experience inform us that the laws of medicine do not vary from state to state in anything like the manner our public law does.

The court held that each Mississippi physician may be expected to have reasonable access to such medical knowledge as is commonly possessed or reasonably available to minimally competent physicians in the same specialty or general field of practice throughout the United States.

Courts sometimes even substitute their judgment for medical judgment. For example, in Helling v. Carey,[11] the Supreme Court of Washington held that compliance with the standards of the profession of ophthalmology, which did not require a routine pressure test for glaucoma to be administered to persons under 40 years of age because their incidence of the disease was extremely low, should not insulate the defendants from liability for failing to give such a test to a patient when the patient's complaints and symptoms should have caused the physician to suspect glaucoma. The court performed a risk-benefit analysis and concluded that the test was a simple and inexpensive one. The court ignored the costs of false-positives and the fact that little evidence exists that early treatment halts the progression of glaucoma.[12]

Courts have also expanded malpractice liability by creating or approving other, sometimes novel, theories of liability, such as negligent infliction of mental distress or an intentional tort (a *tort* is a civil wrong), such as when a physician deliberately alters rec-

---

11. 519 P.2d 981 (Wash. 1974).
12. Furrow et al., pp. 161-62.

ords to create misleading entries or has knowingly made a false material representation to a plaintiff. For example, Simcuski v. Saeli[13] approved of an action for a fraudulent misrepresentation where a physician negligently injured a nerve in a plaintiff's neck and then falsely told her that her postoperative pains were transient and would disappear if she would undertake a physiotherapy regimen. Another judicial innovation is the relatively new cause of action for loss or reduction in a plaintiff's chances of survival in which the plaintiff or his or her heirs can be compensated for negligence that reduced the plaintiff's chances of survival for a particular condition.[14]

Courts have also extended malpractice liability to healthcare facilities in several different ways. For example, until recently, the doctrine of charitable immunity protected nonprofit hospitals from liability for the acts of their employees. Most states have now done away with charitable immunity entirely, although some retain immunity to the extent of statutory ceilings on damages or for charity care only.[15]

In addition, the courts have expanded facility malpractice liability from including only the acts of its employees to including the acts of others who perform medical services for the facility. Traditionally, hospitals were not liable for malpractice committed by independent contractors. However, courts have increasingly found independent contractors to be "employees" for purposes of hospital liability. If, for example, the contract gives the hospital substantial control over the physician's activities, a court might find him or her to be an employee even though the contract calls the physician an independent contractor.[16]

Other courts have found a hospital liable for the acts of an independent contractor when the hospital holds itself out as offering the services to the patient through a physician, particularly in emergency rooms and radiology labs. For example, in Jackson

---

13. 377 N.E.2d 713 (N.Y. 1978).
14. *See, for example,* Herskovits v. Group Health Cooperative of Puget Sound, 664 P.2d 474 (1983).
15. Furrow et al., pp. 222-23.
16. *Id.,* p. 226. *See, for example,* Mduba v. Benedictine Hospital, 384 N.Y.S.2d 527 (3d Dept. 1976).

v. Power,[17] the Supreme Court of Alaska found that a hospital could be liable for emergency room care provided by an emergency room physician who was an independent contractor rather than an employee because the hospital had a nondelegable duty to provide nonnegligent physician care in its emergency room. The plaintiff did not allege that the hospital was negligent in the selection, retention, or supervision of the doctor. Nonetheless, the court found that the hospital could be liable because a jury could find that the plaintiff reasonably believed that the doctor was employed by the hospital to deliver emergency room service. Another case summed up the doctrine well:

> Where a hospital holds itself out to the public as providing a given service, in this instance, emergency services, and where the hospital enters into a contractual arrangement with one or more physicians to direct and provide the service, and where the patient engages the services of the hospital without regard to the identity of a particular physician and where as a matter of fact the patient is relying upon the hospital to deliver the desired health care and treatment, the doctrine of respondeat superior applies and the hospital is vicariously liable for damages proximately resulting from the neglect, if any, of such physicians.[18]

Of course, a facility may be directly liable for negligence in maintaining its facilities; providing and maintaining medical equipment; hiring, supervising, and retaining professional staff; and failing to have in place procedures to protect patients. It must have minimum facility and support systems to treat the range of problems and side effects that may accompany the procedures it offers.[19]

Finally, the zenith (or nadir, depending on your point of view) of the courts' expansion of malpractice liability to institutions was reached in Darling v. Charleston Community Memorial Hospital[20] and its progeny. In the Darling case, the Supreme Court of Illinois expanded vicarious liability doctrine by imposing corporate negligence liability on the hospital regardless of whether medical per-

---
17. 743 P.2d 1376 (Alaska 1987).
18. Hardy v. Brantley, 471 So. 358 (Miss. 1985).
19. Furrow et al., pp. 239-40.
20. 211 N.E.2d 253 (Ill. 1966).

sonnel who were negligent were employees or independent contractors. The court noted:

> The conception that the hospital does not undertake to treat the patient, does not undertake to act through its doctors and nurses, but undertakes instead simply to procure them to act upon their own responsibility, no longer reflects the fact. Present day hospitals . . . regularly employ on a salary basis a large staff of physicians, nurses, and interns, as well as administrative and manual workers, and they charge patients for medical care and treatment. Certainly the person who avails himself of "hospital facilities" expects that the hospital will attempt to cure him, not that its nurses or other employees will act on their own responsibility. The Standards for Hospital Accreditation, the state licensing regulations, and the defendant's own bylaws demonstrate that the medical profession and other responsible authorities regard it as both desirable and feasible that a hospital assume certain responsibilities for the care of the patient.

The next expansion may be extending vicarious liability to managed care organizations, such as health maintenance organizations, although some state legislatures have immunized health services corporations, including HMOs, against tort liability.[21]

The courts' role in the regulation of the healthcare industry will probably only continue to grow. As the legislatures enact more statutes regulating health care and the administrative agencies likewise promulgate more regulations, the courts will be kept busy interpreting them. Further, no letup in the malpractice litigation "crisis" appears likely in the near future. And as healthcare costs continue to rise, causing even more governmental regulation, more and more disputes between individuals and facilities and between competing facilities will ultimately end up in court. A knowledge of how the judicial system "regulates" health care—especially how your facility may be "corporately" liable for the malpractice of a practitioner—will assist you as a financial manager in budgeting for risk management, malpractice insurance, and other activities to protect the facility's financial health.

---

21. Furrow et al., pp. 273-81.

Regulation Through Taxation

The IRS is another government entity that influences the operation of healthcare facilities. For example, nonprofit hospitals have to comply with certain requirements in order to maintain their not-for-profit status and qualify for tax exemption. Requirements for exemption from state taxes vary among the states and depend on the particular type of taxation (income, property, and so on) involved. Exemption from federal corporate income taxation is governed by the Internal Revenue Code (IRC), particularly § 501(c)(3) which specifies the qualifications that allow contributions to the tax-exempt organizations to be tax deductible for the donor, which has obvious importance for fund raising.

Other than the advantage in fund raising inherent in contributions being tax-deductible, a healthcare facility that qualifies for tax-exempt status is exempt from income tax except for income from an unrelated trade or business. Some tax-exempt organizations may also be exempt from federal excise taxes and qualify as issuers of tax-exempt bonds.[1] Further, services performed by an employee of a qualified 501(C)(3) organization are excluded from

---

1. BNA Management Portfolio, *Tax Exempt Organizations: Organization, Operation and Reporting Requirements*, 3d ed. (Washington, D.C.: Bureau of National Affairs, 1990), A-2, citing I.R.C. § 5276(d) (occupational tax); § 4041(g)(4) (diesel fuel tax); § 103 (gross income does not include interest on state and local bonds).

the application of the Federal Unemployment Tax Act,[2] if the entity provides unemployment insurance coverage for its employees, either through a state or through self-insurance.

Other benefits of tax-exempt status include

- ❖ Availability of tax-deferred annuities for employees under IRC § 403(b)
- ❖ Eligibility for deferred compensation plans under IRC § 457
- ❖ Preferential postage rates[3]

The primary disadvantage of qualifying as a tax-exempt organization is that the relevant tax code provisions carry strict operational and organizational requirements that must be complied with in order to maintain tax-exempt status. Under these tests, critical tax issues concerning not-for-profit providers include not only whether the entity qualifies for charitable status but also the effect of the receipt of unrelated taxable business income and the prohibition against private inurement and against lobbying or campaign activities.

❖ Charitable Purposes

To qualify for 501(c)(3) status, a hospital or other healthcare facility must meet two tests:

- ❖ An organizational test requiring that the facility's charter limit it to exempt purposes. The IRS requires the purpose described in the organizational document to contain all three of the following provisions:
  - ❖ that the purposes of the organization are limited to one or more of the specific purposes listed in § 501(c)(3)

---

2. I.R.C. § 3306(c)(8).
3. Bruce R. Hopkins, *The Law of Tax-Exempt Organizations*, 5th ed. (New York: Academy of Political Science, 1987), § 2.2, pp. 32–36.

- that the organization is not expressly empowered to engage in activities that are not in furtherance of one or more of the exempt purposes, unless they are an insubstantial part of its activities
- that upon dissolution of the organization, its assets will be distributed for exempt purposes[4]

❖ An operational test. This test requires the facility to be operated primarily for exempt purposes, such as "charitable," "religious," or "educational" purposes. The presence of one substantial nonexempt purpose is sufficient to deny or revoke tax-exempt status.[5]

For example, in Federation Pharmacy Service, Inc. v. Commissioner[6] the tax court held that a pharmacy that sold drugs at cost to elderly and handicapped patients—with no commitment to use the excess receipts from other sales to provide below-cost or no-cost drugs to the elderly or handicapped—engaged in a substantial nonexempt purpose and was not entitled to tax-exempt status.

Some not-for-profit facilities qualify for their tax-exempt status as religious organizations. Others must qualify as charities. The promotion of health is a community benefit that falls clearly within the charitable category of exempt purposes.[7] This qualification has become more difficult as not-for-profit hospitals have responded to increased competition and cost containment pressures by engaging in strategies that are similar to those used by for-profit providers.[8]

Utah County v. Intermountain Health Care, Inc.,[9] is a good example of the tension between tax-exempt status and competition with for-profit entities. Intermountain Health Care was a nonprofit organization that owned and operated or leased 21 hospitals. The Utah State Tax Commission exempted two hospitals owned by

---
4. Treas. Reg. § 1.501(c)(3)-(1)(b)(1)(i),(1)(b)(6).
5. Dumaine Farms v. Commissioner, 73 T.C. 650, 663 (1980).
6. 72 T.C. 687 (1979).
7. I.R.C. § 100.2.3 17; Rev. Rul. 69-545, 1969-2 C.B. 117, 118.
8. Furrow et al., pp. 457-59.
9. 709 P.2d 265 (Utah 1985).

Intermountain from ad valorem property taxes. On appeal, even though Intermountain contended that the great expense of hospital care and the widespread availability of insurance and government healthcare subsidies made the concept of a hospital supported solely by charity an anachronism, the Supreme Court of Utah found that the tax exemption was not constitutionally permissible, largely because the value of services given away as charity by these two hospitals constituted less than 1 percent of their gross revenues. Nor did the record demonstrate that the hospital's services substantially lessened the burdens of government. After the case, Intermountain agreed to expand its charitable services significantly—by providing charity care in excess of taxes it would otherwise owe and by opening clinics for the homeless and poor in rural areas and on Indian reservations—in return for retaining its tax-exempt status.

Intermountain's case is illustrative of the states' trend to scrutinize the tax-exemption of healthcare facilities more closely, focusing on the amount of charity care they provide. The theory of the tax exemptions is that they are a *quid pro quo* for charitable entities undertaking functions and services the state would otherwise be required to perform.[10]

A hospital seeking tax-exempt status must meet the following tests:

❖ It must be organized as a nonprofit charitable organization for the purpose of operating a hospital for the care of the sick.

❖ It must be operated to the extent of its financial ability for those not able to pay for the services rendered and not exclusively for those who are able and expected to pay. The IRS manual for examination of tax-exempt organizations instructs agents to determine whether "admission is denied to patients because of inability to pay. If so determine whether the class of persons benefiting directly from the hospital's activities is so small that there is no benefit to the community."[11]

---

10. Furrow et al., pp. 459-67.
11. *Id.*, p. 468.

- It must not restrict the use of its facilities to a particular group of physicians and surgeons, such as a medical partnership or association, to the exclusion of all other qualified doctors.
- Its net earnings must not inure directly or indirectly to the benefit of any private shareholder or individual. This prohibition includes payment of excessive salaries, rent, or the use of hospital facilities to serve private interests. No dividends may be either authorized or paid.[12] See the discussion on private inurement later in the chapter.

Alternate delivery systems have received 501(c)(3) status. Consider the situation of the staff model health maintenance organization (HMO). In staff model HMOs, physicians are members of a partnership or corporation that contracts with the HMO to provide services for members on a capitation basis. An HMO received 501(c)(3) status because, in addition to providing services to its members, the HMO offered emergency medical services at its clinic to all persons regardless of ability to pay and also provided other charity care.[13] However, in another case, the IRS refused such status when the HMO did not provide emergency services.[14] The IRS has indicated it will evaluate the tax status of preferred provider organizations (PPOs) under the same standards as HMOs.[15] However, HMOs have had little success in obtaining state tax exemptions.

❖ Unrelated Business Income

As noted earlier, not-for-profit healthcare providers compete with for-profit providers as well as with other not-for-profit providers. Thus, the nonprofit facilities increasingly engage in strategies similar to those used by for-profit facilities. These strategies, such as diversification through joint ventures, raise serious tax concerns.

---

12. Rev. Rul. 56-185, 1956-1 C.B. 202.
13. Sound Health Association v. Commissioner, 71 T.C. 158 (1978).
14. Gen. Couns. Mem. 39057 (Nov. 9, 1983).
15. Gen. Couns. Mem. 39799 (Oct. 25, 1989). *See generally* Furrow et al., pp. 472-74.

A federally tax-exempt organization must be organized primarily for exempt purposes but may engage in some nonexempt business activities. The earnings from such activities are taxable as *unrelated business taxable income (UBTI)*, which the IRS defines as "any trade or business the conduct of which is not substantially related to the exercise of the organization of its charitable purpose or function constituting the basis for its exemption under section 501."[16] In other words, where the production of goods or performance of services from which the facility derives the income contributes importantly to the accomplishment of the exempt purposes, those activities are substantially related to the exempt purposes.[17]

For example, in a private letter ruling, the IRS found that a tax-exempt entity that operated two acute-care community hospitals did not generate UBTI when it operated a magnetic resonance imaging (MRI) system because the MRI system is a unique tool that is important in diagnosing and treating disorders common to patients of the two hospitals. Thus, the MRI system did not jeopardize the 501(c)(3) status of the facilities because it contributed importantly to the accomplishment of the entities' tax-exempt purposes.[18]

Note, however that § 513 provides that "the furnishing by a qualified hospital at or near cost, of certain common services to small hospitals (those with facilities for a maximum of 100 inpatients)" is excluded from the unrelated business income tax if the services assist the small hospitals in performing their exempt functions.[19] Those services include data processing; purchasing; warehousing; billing and collection; food, clinical, industrial engineering, laboratory, printing, communications, record center, and personal services; and the selection, testing, training, and education of personnel.[20]

The IRS has become more aggressive of late in collecting tax on unrelated business income of tax-exempt organizations. As facilities continue to try to compete with other providers and to contain costs, this form of regulation is likely to remain a problem area for some time to come.

---

16. I.R.C. § 513.
17. Treas. Reg. § 1.513-1(d)(2).
18. Priv. Ltr. Rul. 9024085 (Mar. 22, 1990).
19. I.R.C. § 513(e); Treas. Reg. § 1.513-6.
20. I.R.C. § 501(e)(1)(A).

❖ Private Inurement

As noted earlier, a not-for-profit hospital is organized primarily to provide a service to patients. This type of facility may not distribute income to members, directors, or officers.[21] However, a not-for-profit hospital can still pay a reasonable compensation to its corporate members, directors, or officers for their service to the corporation. The nonprofit hospital uses its profits and reinvests its income for institutional purposes.[22]

Section 501(c)(3) of the Internal Revenue Code provides that "no part of the net income [of the exempt organization shall inure] to the benefit of any private shareholder or individual." *Private inurement* is the receipt of financial benefit, other than reasonable payment for services rendered or goods provided, at the expense of the tax-exempt entity.[23] Violation of the prohibition against private inurement can result in the loss of tax-exempt status.

One reason for monitoring the private inurement of not-for-profit hospitals stems from the fact that unlike a for-profit organization, which has an obligation toward its shareholders or owners, a not-for-profit organization tends to distribute its earnings to management or other institutional decision makers.[24]

The *IRS Manual* lists several areas in a nonprofit hospital's operation that should be carefully monitored to ensure that the hospital is not participating in inurement of income or the serving of private interests. First, the manual suggests that the board of trustees or directors and the key member of the administrative medical staff be identified.[25] The manual also suggests the following[26]:

❖ Examine any business relationships or dealings with the hospital.

---

21. LeBlang and Basanta, p. 297.
22. *Id.*, p. 298.
23. Gen. Couns. Mem. 39498 (Apr. 24, 1986).
24. Furrow et al., p. 511.
25. Examination Procedures for Charitable Organizations (Hospitals), *IRS Manual* 4/14/89, Part VII ch. 300 Section 330.3.
26. *Id.*

- Note any pertinent transactions in which supplies or services are provided at prices exceeding competitive market or at preferred terms.
- Be alert for any loan agreements in which interest charged is less than prevailing interest rates.
- Scrutinize any business arrangements under which hospitals finance the construction of medical buildings owned by staff doctors on favorable financial terms that result in private benefit.
- Determine whether any part of the hospital's property (facilities, space, and equipment) or services are used by or rented to doctors or others (such as x-ray and laboratory facilities, pharmacy departments, laundry services, or office space).
- Once copies of pertinent leases and contracts are obtained, it must be determined whether the exempt purpose or private interests are being served or whether liability for an unrelated business tax exists.
- To determine whether private interests are being served in lease transactions, one must ascertain whether the lease payment represents the fair rental value.

Under the IRS's General Counsel Memorandum 37789, "if an organization serves a public interest and also serves a private interest other than incidentally, it is not entitled to exemption under Section 501(c)(3)." The IRS thus analyzes whether a private benefit is incidental by using a qualitative and quantitative approach. The qualitative test recognizes that the exempt purpose of an organization is to provide substantial benefits for the public and that it cannot achieve this purpose without certain private individuals benefiting to an incidental extent. The other test, the quantitative test, requires that the benefits received by the individual or entity must be insubstantial when compared to the public benefit for the organization.[27]

---

27. *See* Priv. Ltr. Rul. 8541108 (July 19, 1985); Gen. Couns. Mem. 39598 (Dec. 8, 1986).

In one case, for example, the IRS reviewed a physician recruitment agreement and found that it would violate the prohibition against private inurement. The hospital guaranteed newly recruited physicians an annual income for two years through a system of subsidies with no obligation to repay any subsidies except out of income earned in excess of the guaranteed annual income. The hospital offered this guaranteed income when necessary to persuade a physician to locate his or her practice in the hospital's service area.

Although the IRS recognized that the hospital had to offer inducements to attract qualified physicians and could offer reasonable compensation without violating the inurement prohibitions, not all the subsidies constituted reasonable compensation. The method of determining the amount of subsidies bore no direct relation to the value of the physician to the hospital. Rather, they were related to the physician's performance in his or her private medical practice. Thus, the IRS concluded that amounts to be paid—and possibly not repaid—as subsidies fell outside the range of reasonable compensation for the benefit to the facility for the doctor's relocation and resulted in inurement of the hospital's net earnings to the recruited physicians.[28]

❖ Restrictions on Lobbying and Campaign Activities

To keep tax-exempt status, public charities are prohibited from substantial legislative activities and from electioneering.[29] Such an entity may elect to engage in insubstantial legislative activities,[30] but the IRS may tax excess expenditures to influence legislation.[31]

❖ Regulation of For-Profit Entities Through Taxation

Not only do taxing authorities regulate nonprofit healthcare providers, they also regulate, directly or indirectly, for-profit pro-

---

28. Gen. Couns. Mem. 39498 (Apr. 24, 1986).
29. Treas. Reg. § 1.501(c)(3)-1(c)(3).
30. I.R.C. § 501(h).
31. *Id.*, § 504.

viders. The issue of what form of business organization to use has tax consequences. Except for Subchapter S corporations, the income from for-profit corporations is doubly taxed, both as income to the corporation and—if distributed to shareholders as dividends—as part of shareholders' individual income. In Subchapter S corporations (small, closely held corporations) the shareholders may elect to be taxed directly on corporate income without imposition of a corporate tax. In partnerships, partnership income is not subject to a partnership tax, but rather the distributions to the partners are taxed as income to them.

As you can see, the federal government and the states regulate the healthcare industry through the tax consequences of, among others, qualifying for tax-exempt financing, the tax consequences of gifts and bequests, taxation of employees, tax aspects of pension plans, and so on. Of course, in these and other tax situations, the entity must comply with the tax statutes and IRS regulations to avoid greater tax liability. Whether or not this pervasive regulation of the provision of health care through taxation is desirable, little doubt exists that financial managers must be familiar with the tax consequences of the facility's operations.

Critical Issues in Healthcare Regulation

In one sense, all issues in health care are "critical." If a medicolegal decision determines whether a particular patient receives a life-saving treatment, that issue is certainly critical to the patient. And a regulatory decision may be critical to a facility if, for example, it determines whether the facility loses its licensure or cannot raise necessary funding without jeopardizing its tax-exempt status. However, certain issues, because of their general applicability, qualify as critical to financial managers in today's healthcare environment. They are raised in this chapter for your further contemplation.

❖ AIDS Issues

The acquired immunodeficiency syndrome (AIDS) epidemic has a number of legal issues that can affect a healthcare financial manager:

- ❖ Liability for transmission of the human immunodeficiency virus (HIV) to patients or to staff
- ❖ Liability for improper disclosure of HIV status

- ❖ The cost of protecting healthcare workers and patients from contracting the disease
- ❖ Antidiscrimination laws requiring facilities to treat AIDS patients, prohibiting discrimination in hiring, and so on
- ❖ Whether the facility can legally test staff for the HIV antibody

❖ Antitrust Issues

The purpose of the antitrust laws is to prohibit business practices that impede competition for goods and services. The federal government and most states have antitrust statutes, and the common law prohibits unfair competition. Since 1975, the government has increasingly regulated the healthcare industry under the antitrust laws. Critical antitrust issues include

- ❖ Whether the denial, suspension, or revocation of staff privileges is to prevent a healthcare professional from competing
- ❖ Whether a private accreditation or professional organization's practices constitute a boycott or otherwise restrain trade and commerce
- ❖ Whether mergers, acquisitions, or other interinstitutional arrangements substantially lessen competition or tend to create a monopoly
- ❖ Whether setting prices for medical or other healthcare services or products constitutes illegal price fixing

Sanctions for antitrust violations include criminal penalties; civil penalties, including treble damages; injunctive relief; adverse tax consequences; and bad publicity and legal costs. For a detailed guide to antitrust laws, see *The Healthcare Financial Manager's Guide to Antitrust Law Issues*.

❖ Environmental and Occupational Safety and Health Issues

Because of public outcry over infectious waste that washed up on the east coast's beaches and because of the seriousness of the AIDS epidemic, both the federal government and the states have become far more aggressive in regulating healthcare providers' medical waste and other environmental and occupational safety and health problems. Healthcare environmental law concerns include

- ❖ Proper disposal of medical waste
- ❖ Protection of staff and patients from AIDS and hepatitis B infection
- ❖ Liability for transferring or acquiring environmentally contaminated property
- ❖ Compliance with the Occupational Safety and Health Act (OSHA)

As in antitrust law, the cost of environmental or occupational safety and health problems can be very high. Such costs may include criminal and civil penalties along with the other costs of lawsuits and, perhaps more importantly, the costs of compliance with environmental regulation. For more information, see *The Healthcare Financial Manager's Guide to Environmental Law Issues.*

❖ Medicare and Medicaid Issues

Obviously, Medicare and Medicaid reimbursement is a critical concern of healthcare financial managers as well as to those seeking benefits under these programs. Medicare and Medicaid issues include

- ❖ Whether a particular item or service will be covered for a beneficiary.

- Whether a provider qualifies for reimbursement under these programs.
- Whether a particular practice violates the fraud and abuse laws or falls within one of the "safe harbors." For more information, see *The Healthcare Financial Manager's Guide to Fraud, Waste, and Abuse Issues and Safe Harbors.*

❖ Other Issues

Other medicolegal issues may also arise but may not affect financial managers as directly as those discussed earlier in the chapter. "Hot" healthcare law issues, other than those discussed in previous chapters, include

- Human reproduction and birth issues, such as genetic screening and engineering, sterilization, artificial insemination, and abortion
- Life and death issues, such as defining death, the "right to die," and do-not-resuscitate orders
- Medical experimentation
- Regulation of drugs and medical equipment
- Mental health issues
- Transplants and anatomical gifts
- Patients' rights

❖ Conclusion

No, you really don't have to be a lawyer to be a healthcare financial manager! However, a familiarity with the regulation of the healthcare industry can make you a better financial manager by helping you to recognize and control the costs of both complying and failing to comply with all the statutes, regulations, court decisions, and other regulatory mechanisms that affect your facility. In addition, you can use your knowledge of the regulatory system to attempt to influence pending legislation or regulations by working with associations such as the Healthcare Financial Management Association, American Hospital Association, and others to make certain the legislature and other entities regulating health care do so with full knowledge of the effects of their actions on the industry.

Glossary

Accreditation Manual for Hospitals   The publication containing the JCAHO's standards for accreditation for hospitals.

Adjudication   The resolution of a dispute in an administrative hearing rather than in a judicial proceeding.

Administrative Agency   A government body other than a legislative or judicial body, such as the U.S. Department of Health and Human Services, that executes governmental policy in a particular area.

Administrative Regulation   A rule issued by an administrative agency to regulate the area in which the agency was created to execute government policy. A regulation ranks below a statute but still has the force of law.

Agency   *See* Administrative Agency.

Antitrust   The body of law intended to protect trade and commerce from unlawful restraints and monopolies.

Articles of Incorporation   The document creating a corporation and defining its powers.

Association   A group of individuals who have joined together for some purpose. The group may be incorporated or unincorporated.

Bill of Rights The first ten amendments to the U.S. Constitution, including such rights as the freedom of speech, of the press, from unreasonable searches and seizures, the right to due process of law, and so on.

Bylaws Rules for the internal government and organization of a corporation or other entity.

Certificate of Need A permit to open a new facility, to expand an existing one, or to purchase expensive medical equipment, granted by state agencies upon a demonstrated need for the facility or equipment.

Charity An entity organized and operated primarily for benevolent, religious, or educational purposes, including providing health care for the needy.

Commerce Clause The portion of the U.S. Constitution that permits the federal government to regulate trade that moves between the states.

Corporation An artificial person composed of individuals (shareholders), which normally has perpetual duration and the capacity to exercise the powers in its articles of incorporation that are not illegal.

Credentialing The act of approving a healthcare professional's access to healthcare facilities. The granting of hospital or other related privileges.

Credentials Committee A committee of the medical staff that recommends whether a practitioner should receive medical staff privileges and investigates charges of poor performance.

Diversity of Citizenship A ground for federal court jurisdiction involving suits between citizens of different states when the amount involved is greater than $50,000.

Due Process The constitutional right that the government will not deprive any person (or entity) of life, liberty, or property without giving notice of the proposed action and an opportunity to be heard.

Equal Protection The legal concept, embodied in the Fourteenth Amendment, which prevents the government from treating persons differently (discriminating) for no good reason.

Fiduciary A person or entity who holds a position of trust or confidence and must be both loyal and responsible, such as a trustee.

Fourteenth Amendment The amendment to the U.S. Constitution that makes the Bill of Rights applicable to the states and guarantees citizens of the states the equal protection of the laws.

Fraud and Abuse Laws Federal laws that attempt to police healthcare provider conduct to control costs while protecting quality. They make certain practices, such as receiving kickbacks for referrals, felonies.

Governing Board The board of directors (trustees) of a healthcare facility. The group that directs the policy of the institution.

Health and Human Services The federal agency responsible for health policy.

Health Care Financing Administration The component of the U.S. Department of Health and Human Services responsible for the Medicaid program.

Health Maintenance Organization (HMO) An entity that provides comprehensive healthcare services to its membership for a fixed, per capita fee.

Hospital Administrator The chief executive officer of a hospital.

Incorporation The act of forming a corporation.

Independent Contractor A person who agrees to work for another but who is not controlled by the other as distinguished from an employee.

Injunction A court order directing a person to do or to refrain from doing something.

Inurement *See* Private Inurement.

JCAHO Acronym for Joint Commission on the Accreditation of Healthcare Organizations.

Joint Commission on the Accreditation of Healthcare Organizations A private, nonprofit association whose purpose is to improve the quality of health care through a voluntary accreditation process.

Jurisdiction The power to hear and decide a case.

Licensure The act of authorizing a professional or an entity, such as a doctor or a hospital, to practice.

Malpractice *See* Medical Malpractice.

Medicaid The federal program to provide medical care to the indigent. However, the states, not the federal government, administer the program and receive federal funds for many of their programs.

Medical Malpractice A breach of the legally required standard of care by a physician or other healthcare professional—the negligent rendition of health care.

Medical Staff An organized body of physicians or other healthcare professionals whom the governing board has authorized to practice their profession in the facility within the scope of their delineated clinical privileges.

Medical Waste Any waste generated by a healthcare provider.

Medicare The federal program intended to ensure adequate health care for the aged.

Medicare Utilization and Quality Peer Review Program A federal program that attempts to police the utilization and quality of Medicare-financed care.

Merger A consolidation of corporations in which only one of two or more survives or that brings a new corporation into being, ending the existence of the former ones.

Monopoly The absolute control, by one entity, of the purchase, sale, manufacture, or use of a particular good or service.

Negligence A tort involving the failure to use due care by one who has a duty to do so.

Occupational Safety and Health Act The major federal statute requiring employers to provide a safe and healthy work environment.

Partnership An association of two or more persons to carry on as co-owners a business for profit.

Peer Review The scrutiny of healthcare professionals by those with similar credentials to determine whether they should have access to healthcare facilities.

Police Power The inherent power of state governments to impose restrictions on individuals or entities that are reasonably related to the promotion and maintenance of the health, safety, morals, and general welfare of the public.

Preemption The legal doctrine under which a federal law prevails over a state law when the two conflict.

Preferred Provider Organization A series of contracts between third-party payers, subscribers, and healthcare providers that encourages subscribers to avoid nonparticipating physicians.

Private Inurement The receipt of financial benefit, other than reasonable payment for services rendered or goods provided, from a tax-exempt entity.

Professional Corporation A corporation whose shareholders are all licensed professionals, such as physicians. Normally, shareholders are only liable to the extent of their own investment in the corporation and are not liable for the negligent acts of others.

Quality Assurance The evaluation of the quality and appropriateness of patient care.

Regulation *See* Administrative Regulation.

Risk Management A program to reduce medical malpractice and its associated costs by ensuring practitioners are qualified, instituting quality assurance procedures, obtaining proper insurance, and so on.

Safe Harbor An innocuous payment practice that is clearly and always acceptable and that will not be treated as a violation of the fraud and abuse laws under regulations promulgated by the Office of the Inspector General, U.S. Department of Health and Human Services.

Statute A law enacted by a legislature.

Subpoena A court order commanding a person to appear at trial or to bring certain documents in the person's custody or possession to a place the subpoena specifies.

Supremacy Clause The portion of the U.S. Constitution that makes federal law prevail over (preempt) state law when they conflict.

Tort A civil—as opposed to a criminal—wrong, such as malpractice or other negligence.

Unrelated Business Income Money received from the sale of goods or the provision of services that are not related to the tax-exempt purposes of a nonprofit entity.

Utilization Review The act of determining whether medical care was appropriate or properly performed.

Bibliography

BNA Management Portfolio. *Tax Exempt Organizations: Organization, Operation and Reporting Requirements*, 3d ed. Washington, D.C.: Bureau of National Affairs, 1990.

Caruso, Aaron R. "The Time Present Foundation of the Maryland Medical Professional Regulation," *Courts, Health Science & The Law* 1, No. 2 (October 1990).

Feldman, Penny, and Marc Roberts. "Magic Bullets or Seven Card Stud: Understanding Health Care Regulation," in Richard S. Gordon, ed., *Issues in Health Care Regulation*. New York: McGraw-Hill Book Co., 1980.

Furrow, Barry R., Sandra H. Johnson, Timothy S. Jost, and Robert L. Schwartz. *Health Law, Cases, Materials and Problems*, 2d ed. St. Paul, Minn.: West Publishing Co., 1991.

Gordon, Richard S., ed. *Issues in Health Care Regulation*. New York: McGraw-Hill Book Co., 1980.

Grad, Frank P., and Noelia Marti. *Physician's Licensure and Discipline*. Dobbs Ferry, N.Y.: Ocean Publications, 1979.

Hopkins, Bruce R. *The Law of Tax-Exempt Organizations*, 5th ed. New York: Academy of Political Science, 1987.

Huffman, Edna. *Medical Record Management*, 9th ed. Berwyn, Ill.: Physician's Record Co., 1990.

Joint Commission on Accreditation of Healthcare Organizations. *Accreditation Manual for Hospitals, 1991*. Chicago: JCAHO, 1990.

Jones, Harry W., John M. Kernochan, and Arthur W. Murphy. *Legal Method: Cases and Text Materials*. Mineola, N.Y.: The Foundation Press, 1980.

Jost, Timothy S. "The Joint Commission on the Accreditation of Hospitals: Private Regulation of Health Care and the Public Interest." *Boston College Law Review* XXIV, No. 4 (July 1983).

Kellie, Shirley, and John Kelley, "Medicare Peer Review Organization Preprocedure Review Criteria," *Journal of the American Medical Association* 265 (March 13, 1991), pp. 1265-70.

LeBlang, Theodore, and W. Eugene Basanta. *The Law of Medical Practice in Illinois*. Rochester, N.Y.: Lawyer Co-operative Publishing Co., 1986, and 1992 Cumulative Supplement.

Levin, Arthur. "The Search for New Forms of Control," in *Regulating Health Care: The Struggle for Control*. New York: Academy of Political Science, 1980.

Miller, Robert. *Problems in Hospital Law*. Rockville, Md.: Aspen Systems Corp., 1983.

Morter, Christopher. "The Health Care Quality Improvement Act of 1986: Will Physicians Find Peer Review More Inviting?" *Virginia Law Review* 74 (September 1988).

Popko, Kathleen M. *Regulatory Controls: Implications for the Community Hospital*. Lexington, Mass.: Lexington Books, 1976.

Roemer, Ruth, and George McKray, eds. *Legal Aspects of Health Policy, Issues and Trends*. Westport, Conn.: Greenwood, 1980.

Schwartz, Bernard. *Administrative Law*, 2d ed. Boston and Toronto: Little, Brown & Co., 1984.

Steimetz, Karen. "Medical Staff Membership Decisions: Judicial Intervention," *University of Illinois Law Review* (1985).

Stedman, Thomas L. *Stedman's Medical Dictionary*, 24th ed. Baltimore: Williams & Wilkins 1982.

Steele, Charles, and Mary Huff. "Antitrust Issues Related to Health Maintenance Organizations and Preferred Provider Organizations," *Managed Health Care 1988*. New York: Practicing Law Institute, 1988.

Tomes, Jonathan P. *The Healthcare Financial Manager's Guide to Antitrust Law Issues*. Westchester, Ill.: Healthcare Financial Management Association, 1992.

Tomes, Jonathan P. *The Healthcare Financial Manager's Guide to Environmental Law Issues*. Westchester, Ill.: Healthcare Financial Management Association, 1992.

Tomes, Jonathan P. *The Healthcare Financial Manager's Guide to Fraud, Waste, and Abuse Issues and Safe Harbors.* Westchester, Ill.: Healthcare Financial Management Association, 1992.

Unland, James. *The Trustee's Guide to Understanding Hospital Business Fundamentals.* Westchester, Ill.: Healthcare Financial Management Association, 1991.

Index

A
Accreditation Manual for Hospitals (JCAHO), 36
Adjudication defined, 15
Agencies, lawmaking powers of executive, 14–15
AIDS
 as healthcare environmental law issue, 75
 healthcare regulation issues of, 73–74
Alexander v. Choate, 10
Allied medical professionals, specialty certification by, 40–41
Amendments to the Constitution. *See* U.S. Constitution
American Academy of Pediatrics, 41
American Board of Medical Specialties, 29
American College of Surgeons, 36, 40
American College of Surgeons Hospital Standardization Program, 35
American Dental Association (ADA), 36
American Hospital Association (AHA), 36, 40, 77
American Medical Association (AMA), 36
 Council on Medical Education, 40
American Osteopathic Association (AOA), 40
Antitrust issues in healthcare industry, 74
Arrangements, interinstitutional, 74
Articles of incorporation, 43–45, 52
Association
 defined, 18
 professional, 20
 types of, 18

B
Bibliography, 85–87
Board certification, 29
Bradwell v. Illinois, 25
Business Corporation Act, 21
Bylaws, corporate, 43–45

C
Cancer therapy programs, approval of, 40
Carlton v. Herschel, 13
Cash flow, effects of regulation on hospitals', 4
Certificate of authority, 23
Certificate of registration, 19
Certificates of need (CON), 4, 10, 32–33
Certification of healthcare providers, 9, 29
Charitable purposes, tests for, 64–67
Charities, exempt purposes of, 65
Charter, healthcare facility, 64–65
Clinical performance, monitoring and evaluating, 39
Clinical privileges of medical staff, 48
Congress, role in healthcare regulation of U.S., 14–15
Corporation
 defined, 17
 incorporation process for, 43–45
 legal status of, 18
 professional, 19–21
 taxation of, 72
 types of, 18
Cost of medical care, 2
Court(s), 53–61
 of appeal, 54–55
 appellate, 53–55
 federal, 55–56
 federal district, 55–56
 of general jurisdiction, 54
 intermediate appellate, 55
 state, 54–55
 state supreme, 54–55
 supreme judicial, 54

system of, 53–56
trial, 53–55
U.S. Supreme, 55–56
Cross v. Guthery, 57
Cruzan v. Director, Missouri Department of Health, 56

D
Darling v. Charleston Community Memorial Hospital, 40, 60–61
Death issues in healthcare industry, 76
Department of Health and Human Services, U.S., 14
Disciplinary actions, due process in, 29
Doctrine of charitable immunity, 59
Drug testing programs, litigation concerning, 13–14
Drugs, regulation of, 76
Due process, 10–11, 29
Dumaine Farms v. Commissioner, 65

E
Electioneering, 71
Employees
  HIV testing of, 74
  unemployment insurance coverage for, 63–64
Environmental issues, 75
Equal protection, 12
Excise taxes, 63

F
Federal authority to regulate health care, 8–14
Federal government expenditures for health care, 8
Federation Pharmacy Service, Inc. v. Commissioner, 65
Fiduciaries, board members as, 47
Freedom from unreasonable searches and seizures, 13–14
Freedom of speech, 12–13

G
General Not for Profit Corporation Act, 21
Glossary, 79–84
Goldberg v. Kelly, 11
Governing board, hospital, 45–47
Governmental power, process for executing, 14–16

H
Hall v. Hilbun, 57–58
Hardy v. Brantley, 60
Hathaway v. Worcester, 12
Health Care Reimbursement Reform Act of 1985, 23
Health insurance plans prerequisite for payment, 36–37
Health Maintenance Organization Act of 1973, 24
Health maintenance organizations (HMOs), 21
  expansion of malpractice liability to, 61
  federal regulation of, 24
  501(c)(3) status for, 67
  state regulation of, 22–24
Healthcare Financial Management Association, 40, 77
Healthcare industry, overview of legal status of, 1–5
Healthcare professionals
  licensing of, 25–29
  uncompetitive market for entry of, 2
Healthcare regulation
  by Congress, 14–15
  cost control factor in, 2
  by the courts, 53–61
  critical issues in, 73–77
  government justification for, 1–4
  implications of increased, 4–5
  legal basis for government, 7–15
  by licensing organizations, 25–34
  by organizational statutes, 17–24
  by the president, 14–15

by private organizations, 35–41
by taxation, 63–72
Healthcare services, "purchasing," 3
Helling v. Carey, 58
Herskovits v. Group Health
 Cooperative of Puget Sound, 59
Hospital administrator
 authority granted by governing
  board to, 46–48
 JCAHO standards for, 48
 responsibilities of, 48
Hospital Licensing Standards, 30
Hospitals
 charitable purposes tests of, 67
 doctrine of charitable immunity
  for nonprofit, 59
 as for-profit or not-for-profit
  corporations, 18
 inspections of, 36
 lease and rental agreements of, 70
 licensing of, 29–31
 private inurement by not-for-
  profit, 69–71
 taxation of for-profit, 71–72
 tax-exempt status of not-for-profit,
  63–72
 unrelated business income of, 63,
  67–68
Human immunodeficiency virus
 (HIV)
 testing staff for, 74
 transmission, liability for, 73

I
Independent contractors, healthcare
 facility liability for, 59–60
Infection control requirements, 39,
 51
Intermediate sanctions, 31
Internal Revenue Code regulation
 of private inurement in exempt
  organizations, 69–71
 of providers as employers, 9
 of tax deductibility of
  contributions, 63
Internal Revenue Service

General Counsel Memorandum
 37789, 70
influence on operation of
 healthcare facilities, 63
manual for examination of tax-
 exempt organizations, 66, 69
unrelated business taxable income
 (UBTI) defined by, 68
Internships, approval of, 40

J
Jackson v. Power, 60
Jane Doe v. Victory Memorial
 Hospital, et al., 50
Joint Commission on the
 Accreditation of Healthcare
 Organizations (JCAHO), 1, 31,
 35–40
 accreditation standards of, 36, 38–
  40, 43
 categories of service of, 37
 medical staff bylaws specified by,
  44–45
 purpose of, 35
 quality assurance program
  requirements of, 51–52
 representatives of medical
  profession on, 35–36
 surveys by, 37–38
Joint ventures, 67
Judicial system, 53–61
 malpractice litigation in, 57–61
 overview of, 53–56

K
Kemp v. Claiborne County Hospital,
 13–14
Klein v. Califano, 11
Klein v. Department of Registration
 & Education, 29

L
License revocation, 30
Licensing
 of healthcare facilities, 29–31
 of healthcare professionals, 25–29

Lobbying restrictions on tax-exempt charities, 71
Lynch v. Redfield Foundation, 47

M
Magnetic resonance imaging (MRI) equipment, 68
Malpractice liability, expansion of, 57–60
Malpractice litigation, 57–61
Managed care organizations, expansion of malpractice liability to, 61
Marshall v. Barlow's Inc., 13
Mduba v. Benedictine Hospital, 59
Medical Corporation Act, 20
Medical curriculum, 27–28
Medical equipment issues, 76
Medical licensing statutes, 25–34
Medical Practice Act, 19
Medical review criteria, 52
Medical staff
  bylaws, 44–45
  categories of, 49
  responsibilities for quality of services of, 48–49, 51–52
  role in self-regulation of, 48–52
Medicare and Medicaid
  certification of facilities, 31
  fraud and abuse laws, 76
  issues for, in healthcare industry, 75–76
  provider standards, 31
Medicare Utilization and Quality Peer Review (PRO) program, 2, 4
Memorial Hospital v. Maricopa County, 12
Morelli v. Eshan, 21

N
North Carolina v. Califano, 10

O
Occupational safety issues, 75
O'Connor v. Ortega, 13

P
Partnership defined, 18
Patients' rights, 76
Peer review groups, responsibility for staff privileges of, 49–50
Physician specialty board certification, 40–41
Physicians
  hospitals' competition for, 3
  medical association formed by, 20–21
  medical corporations formed by, 19
  negligence by, 57
Preferred provider organizations (PPOs)
  federal regulation of, 24
  501(c)(3) status for, 67
  state regulation of, 23
Preferred terms, examination of, 70
Price fixing, 74
Professional corporation acts, 19–21
Professional Service Corporation Act, 20

Q
Quality assurance
  as factor in reappointments, 39–40, 52
  medical staff responsibility for, 48–49, 51–52
  peer review group's role in, 49–50

R
Rehabilitation Act of 1973, section 504 prohibition of discrimination against the handicapped, 10
Reproduction and birth issues, 76
Residency programs, 37
Rodreiques v. Furtado, 13

S
Searches and seizures, protection from unreasonable, 13–14
Self-regulation, 43–52

Simcuski v. Saeli, 69
Staff privileges, 49, 74. *See also* Medical staff
State courts, regulation of health care by, 54–55
States
  authority to regulate health care by, 7–8, 17
  certificates of need required by most, 32–33
  facility licensing by, 29–31
  hospital governing authority standards issued by some, 46
  JCAHO accreditation accepted by some, 36
  medical license renewal by, 28
  preconditions for medical practice set by, 26–27
  regulation of HMOs and PPOs by, 22–24

T
Taxation, regulation through, 63–72
Technologies, regulation of new, 33
Third-party payers, cost of medical treatment affected by, 3
Thompson v. Division of Health of Missouri, 15, 30
Tort defined, 58
Transcripts of education completed, 26–27
Transplant issues for healthcare industry, 76
Trustees
  as fiduciaries, 47
  staff privileges granted by, 49

U
Uniform Partnership Act, 20–21
Unrelated business income, 63, 67–68
Urine testing, 13–14
U.S. Constitution
  First Amendment, freedom of speech protected by, 12–13
  Fourth Amendment, protection from unreasonable searches and seizures by, 13–14
  Fifth Amendment, due process clause of, 10
  Tenth Amendment, state rights of, 8
  Fourteenth Amendment, due process clause of, 10
  judicial power defined in Article III, Section 2 of, 55
  limits of federal government's regulatory rights under, 9
  supremacy clause of Article VI of, 9–10
Utah County v. Intermountain Health Care, Inc., 65–66
Utilization review requirements, 39, 51

V
Virginia State Board of Pharmacy v. Virginia Citizens Consumer Council, Inc., 12

About the Author

Jonathan P. Tomes is an associate professor at IIT Chicago-Kent College of Law. Among the subjects he has taught is administrative law—the part of the law that deals with the rules and regulations that administrative agencies, such as the Environmental Protection Agency, Health and Human Services, the Occupational Safety and Health Administration, and so forth, issue to control publicly regulated businesses such as healthcare providers and hospital law.

Before going to law school, Professor Tomes served as an infantry platoon leader in Vietnam, where he won the Silver Star and the Combat Infantry Badge among other awards. Then he graduated first in his class at Oklahoma City University School of Law and won the Oklahoma Bar Association outstanding law student award. He is a member of the Illinois and Oklahoma bars. Following graduation, he served in the Judge Advocate General's Corps, U.S. Army, until he retired as a lieutenant colonel in 1988. While in the military, he served as prosecutor, defense counsel, and military judge before becoming Chief of Special Claims, Tort Claims Division, U.S. Army Claims Service, where he was in charge of processing and adjudicating claims that occurred overseas against the military, primarily medical malpractice claims. That assignment led to his interest in healthcare law. The military rewarded his twenty years' service by awarding him the Legion of Merit, the second-highest service award in the military, upon his retirement.

Among Professor Tomes's publications are *The Servicemember's Legal Guide, Healthcare Records: A Practical Legal Guide, The Trustee's Guide to Understanding Healthcare Environmental Law, The*

Trustee's Guide to Understanding Healthcare Antitrust Law, *The Trustee's Guide to Understanding Peer Review and Credentialling*, and articles in the *Boston University Annual Review of Banking Law*, *Richmond Law Review*, *Air Force Law Review* (the U.S. Supreme Court cited his article in this law review), and *The Practical Lawyer*.